DEMCO

THE
WORLD *Mythology*
SERIES

Dragons,
Gods and Spirits
from
Chinese Mythology

DRAGONS, GODS & SPIRITS
from
CHINESE MYTHOLOGY

TEXT BY TAO TAO LIU SANDERS

ILLUSTRATIONS BY JOHNNY PAU

PETER BEDRICK BOOKS

NEW YORK

Peter Bedrick Books
2112 Broadway
New York, NY 10023

Published by agreement with Eurobook Ltd, England

Library of Congress
Cataloging-in-Publication Data
Sanders, Tao Tao Liu
    Dragons, gods & spirits from Chinese mythology /
text by Tao Tao Liu Sanders; illustrations by Johnny Pau.
        p.   cm.
    Originally published by Eurobook Limited, 1980.
    Includes bibliographical references and index.
    ISBN 0-87226-922-1
    1. Mythology, Chinese. I. Title. II. Title: Dragons,
gods and spirits from Chinese mythology.
    BL1802.S26   1994
299′.51—dc20   94-8354

Printed in Italy
5 4 3 2 1 94 95 96 97 98 99

THE AUTHOR
Dr Tao Tao Liu Sanders was born in China but has lived
in England for most of her life. Her researches have been
in the field of Chinese literature, especially poetry. She
lectures in Chinese at the University of Oxford and is
Dean of Wolfson College.

THE ARTIST
Johnny Pau is Chinese and was brought up in Borneo,
where his family still live. He came to England to study
art and now works as a freelance designer and illustrator
in London.

Contents

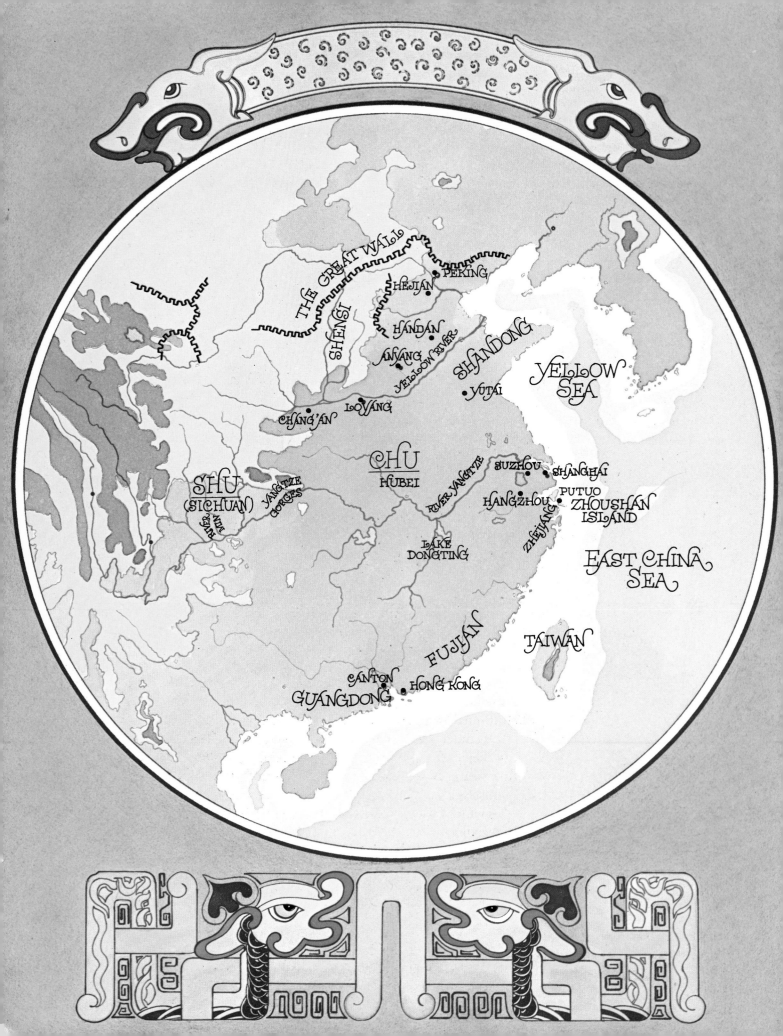

The Chinese World

The land of the Chinese is about the size of Europe and is at least as varied in its scenery and climate. In the north lie the arid plains of the Yellow River with their icy, dry winters and hot humid summers; about two days' journey by rail southwards, the climate is tropical. High mountains lie in the west, where they rise to join the Plateau of Tibet but in most of the rest of China the hills are low, except in the south-east where uplands cut off southern coastal provinces such as Fujian and Canton from the rest of the country. The two great rivers of China rise in the western highlands and flow eastwards to water the great plains of China, discharging into the Yellow Sea and the East China Sea.

The earliest Chinese culture was found in the northern part of present-day China, mainly in the basin of the Yellow River, north to the edge of the plain and south as far as the River Yangtze. This was the land of our earliest mythology, the home of the first people created by the gods.

China's long history is as ancient as that of the Greeks and in many ways parallels Greek development. It began around the twelfth century BC and by the fourth century BC the Chinese, like the Greeks, were already highly civilized. However, unlike the Greeks, whose land was conquered soon afterwards by other races, and whose civilization ceased to develop along its original line, Chinese civilization has continued as an unbroken tradition to the present day.

Of course there were invaders and conquerors who came to China but their cultures were always less developed than the Chinese and they nearly always ended up by being absorbed into Chinese culture themselves. Until modern times the only equally advanced civilization with which the Chinese came into contact was that of the Indians. The two civilizations met peacefully through cultural and trade connections but the encounter had a great effect on China, particularly since it brought with it a new religion—Buddhism.

Before Buddhism, Chinese religion was similar to that of the ancient Greeks, with many different gods representing different aspects of nature, and beliefs which attempted to explain the mysteries of the universe in human terms. Educated men, whilst aware of the possibility of a higher supernatural power, were not religious and did not worship a deity. Instead they lived their lives according to a moral code worked out on human principles.

The most important school of thought, which dominated China for thousands of years, was Confucianism. It is named after the founder of the school, Master Kong or *Kongfuzi,* in roman spelling Confucius. Confucianism was concerned mainly with human relationships and taught a practical social order which enabled people to live in harmony with each other. To balance this worldly outlook another way of thinking developed—Taoism. The word Tao means 'the Way' and Taoism was a mystical search for the laws which govern our lives, taking into account forms of life other than human beings.

These two main systems of thinking were already established when Buddhism came to China. At its highest level Buddhism, too, was an intellectual religion but it brought with it its own gods, spirits and superstitions which were eagerly accepted by the Chinese into their own beliefs. Buddhism also influenced the native Taoism, which now became more involved with religious practices such as a priesthood and monasticism.

Because religions in China developed from many sources, they were a mixture of different beliefs. They were totally unlike a religion such as Christianity which, though it has absorbed some elements from other religions and cults, has retained its basic beliefs in a very pure form. The Christian god rises above all challenge whilst the Chinese deities vie with and jostle each other in heaven as well as on earth. The result is often a fine medley of Buddhist and Taoist elements.

In this book the first four sections following this chapter deal with the early myths of China, myths developed by a simple, robust people, to explain the things they did not understand in the world around them. Then come the folk tales and religious stories of the later civilization. There are no clear cut differences between them, though the later stories come from a more complex and technically more advanced society.

All these stories are now old and some are very ancient indeed, dating back to the eighth to fifth centuries BC. Many have come down to us by word of mouth and there may be several different versions of each one.

This often happens when stories are told instead of being written down. Each time a new teller passes the story on details change, though the outline remains the same. The tales are nearly all familiar to present-day Chinese, who have loved them and told them over and over again to their children. People have ceased to believe in the gods as supernatural powers but many of the religious practices have survived as colourful folk customs such as the Dragon Boat Festival which, like Christmas in the west, provides a welcome holiday from the daily routine.

The Chinese divide their history up into dynasties, each representing the period of time when a particular family ruled as emperors. The last imperial dynasty before the republican era was called Ching and lasted from the seventeenth century to 1911. The Tang dynasty which is often mentioned in these stories was from the seventh to the tenth centuries and was one of the most prosperous and lively periods in Chinese history.

Although the Chinese language has changed radically through the ages, yet Chinese characters, that is written Chinese, have remained the same since about the third century BC when the First Emperor of Chin, the first powerful Chinese despot, is supposed to have standardized the script. We no longer know how the ancient Chinese pronounced the characters but nowadays in standard Chinese pronunciation (also called Mandarin) each character is pronounced as a single syllable with one or two syllables forming a word. Chinese surnames are nearly all one syllable such as Zhang or Li. Given names are often two syllables and are spelled in English as one word.

In this book apart from well-known Chinese names such as Peking and Taoism, the proper names are spelled according to a system invented by the Chinese and used internationally, known by its Chinese name of *pinyin.* If an English-speaking person pronounces the words just as they are written they will sound almost like their correct Chinese pronunciation.

The only exceptions to the *pinyin* system are the sounds which in *pinyin* appear as q (pronounced ch as in cheap) and x (pronounced sh as in sheep); for these we have used the more familiar ch and sh spellings.

Gods from the dawn of time

At the dawn of time the universe was a dark chaos, a black mass of nothingness. Heaven and earth were not separated, neither was night or day. The sun, the moon and the galaxies were all quite unformed. It is almost impossible for human beings to imagine a situation where nothing exists and to make this unimaginable time and place more real, some people thought of it as a large egg. In this dark, egg-like mass was born the first creature of the universe; he was called Pangu.

Pangu grew in all enveloping darkness and slept a sleep lasting several thousands of years. When he woke up at last he had grown into a giant and, realizing that he lived in chaos, he was determined to create order. He took a heavy axe in his hands (though we have no idea where he obtained it) and with a mighty blow split the egg apart. The lighter elements in the egg rose and floated upwards to become the sky; the heavier elements sank downwards to become the earth.

As the elements separated on the impact of his blow, Pangu was afraid that they might close together again so with his hands he pushed the sky farther away, at the same time treading hard upon the earth to keep it well apart from the sky. His strength was such that he pushed the sky farther up by one *zhang* (about ten feet) each day. As the sky retreated farther and farther so Pangu grew taller and taller until finally he stood like a pillar holding up the firmament. For aeons he remained like this until the sky and the earth each in its own way solidified and became firm and there was no longer any danger of their closing together again to become the dark chaos from which they had emerged.

Having completed his task Pangu felt that he could now lie down to take a rest. However, many thousands of years had passed since he had first grown inside the formless egg and he was by now so old in both body and spirit that his sleep grew deeper and deeper and he drifted slowly into death. But Pangu did not return to the darkness from which he had come. As he died, his body changed to create the world as we now know it: his breath turned into wind and clouds, his voice turned into thunder, his left eye turned into the sun and his right eye into the moon. His body and limbs turned into mountain ranges and his blood became flowing rivers. Every part of his anatomy became a part of nature. The hairs on his body turned into trees and flowers, the

parasites living on his skin turned into animals and fishes and his bones formed different kinds of precious stones and minerals. Even his sweat turned into dew.

So the great giant Pangu, the first living thing in the universe, created the world we know, giving everything he owned to the benefit of the earth and to the people who were soon to inhabit it. As for the sky and the earth, they remained separate and apart, although later some people believed that the high mountains formed from Pangu's body acted as pillars to support the blue arch of the heavens.

Although the universe had now taken shape and was complete with sun, moon, mountains, rivers, plants and animals, there were as yet no people. The earth was inhabited in these early times by gods, giants and other monstrous creatures. The most important of the gods was a mother goddess called Nüwa who was a creator and bringer of order. She was shaped like a human being on the upper part of her body, with a human face and human arms, but the lower part of her body was like a dragon's. She was also able to change shape and appeared in many different forms.

Nüwa travelled around the world but though she found it rich and beautiful it was also lonely and desolate for there were no human beings and Nüwa wished for the company of people who could love, feel and think as she did. One day she came to the great Yellow River. From the river bed she scooped out handfuls of mud and shaped little dolls from them; she shaped the head and arms like her own but instead of a dragon tail she gave the dolls legs so that they could walk around upright. She put a great deal of care into the making of these little images and was pleased with the result. Breathing life into them she was delighted to see them spring up and dance around her, shouting joyfully and calling her their mother.

At first Nüwa made the dolls one by one by hand but after she had made a large number in this slow, careful way she decided to use her supernatural powers to achieve a quicker result. She rolled a length of cane in the river mud and as she flicked the cane out onto dry land small drops of mud fell off and were instantly transformed into men and women. Later some people used to say that those whom she shaped with her own hands were the fortunate and well-endowed people of the world whilst those who were formed by the shaking of the length of cane were the poorer and less fortunate people. Eventually, having created enough men and women Nüwa instituted marriage amongst them so that they could procreate and continue the human race without any further help from her.

Nüwa had a companion who is shown in ancient paintings with a similar shape, the head and upper body of a man but the lower limbs of a dragon. His name was Fushi and he, too, was a great benefactor of the human race. The greatest gift of all that he bestowed upon mankind was fire. The humans had seen fire striking from heaven in the form of lightning but it was Fushi who taught them how to harness it for their own use and showed them how to summon it by drilling one piece of dried wood upon another. With fire, the humans could cook their food and need not eat it indigestibly raw. They were also able to hunt more effectively for all wild animals feared the flames—and only man could control them. Some stories say that Fushi was either the son or the brother of the thunder god himself and that was how he was able to pass on his great gift to mankind.

Fushi also taught people to make ropes and nets with which to catch fish but he was not solely concerned with practical arts; he also attended to the humans' spiritual needs by teaching them music and he showed them the mystic art of divination, the foretelling of the future. He was the first to draw up the eight hexagrams, written symbols consisting of solid and broken lines representing eight elemental things of this world. Each hexagram consisted of three short lines. Different arrangements of lines stood for heaven, earth, water, fire, mountain, thunder, wind and river. The symbols, used in combination, had oracular meanings which were later interpreted through a manual of divination known as the *Yijing* or the *Book of Changes*. People in both East and West still consult this ancient book.

Divination was extremely important in those primitive days. People depended on it to foretell the outcome of wars, to forecast the events of

peace and affairs of state and, before modern medicine, to guess the progress of an illness.

The names of Fushi and Nüwa are often linked in ancient writings as the friends of mankind. Some people said that they were brother and sister, others that they were husband and wife. There are also stories that give them a different part to play in the creation of the human race. According to these, long ago the world was inundated by a mighty flood. The only people to escape drowning were a young boy and girl called Fushi and Nüwa who floated to safety in a large gourd. When the flood eventually subsided Fushi and Nüwa were married and with their children the human race began again.

Whatever lies behind the different myths of Fushi and Nüwa, one thing emerges clearly: they were considered to be the original creators of mankind and were our earliest teachers.

After Nüwa had made human beings and Fushi had taught them the skills they needed to lead a civilized existence, humans were able to live in some comfort and security. Then, one day, quite unexpectedly, Gonggong, the God of Water and Zhurong, the God of Fire, suddenly started a fight. No-one knows why the battle began but before long it had become extraordinarily fierce and, raging right out of the boundaries of heaven, it spilled out into the world of men.

After many days of bitter fighting, the God of Fire was victorious. The God of Water, Zhurong, was extremely ashamed of himself, so much so that he dared not meet his fellow gods again and decided to commit suicide. The method he chose had unfortunate results for the world of men for he chose to kill himself by running his head against one of the mountains that acted as pillars to support the universe.

In fact he did himself very little harm (after all, he was a god) but he did a great deal of damage to the mountain he had selected to run against. The great peak of jagged rock tumbled around him, crushing one corner of the world while at the same time the heavens the mountain had supported fell away, leaving a great hole in the blue arch of the sky. Huge crevasses gaped in the shattered earth, some releasing leaping flames, others gushing with water from unknown depths which flooded vast areas of land and turned them into a sea. Thousands of people drowned, thousands more watched helplessly as the tongues of flame burned their houses and crops. Nüwa, the creator and bringer of order, could not stand by and see this terrible devastation and watch her children made fugitives. As quickly as she could, she began to repair the damage.

Out of the river beds of the Yellow River and the Yangtze she carefully selected many pebbles coloured with the five primary colours. These she melted in a heavenly forge and with them she mended the sky so that it was once more a complete, rounded arch. To make sure that the heavens never fell down again she took one of the giant immortal tortoises, chopped off its four legs and stood them as extra supporting pillars at the four points of the compass. She burned reeds from beside the river and with the ashes stuffed up the great crevasses that had opened in the earth and she forced back the flooding water.

According to some sources, to help the people forget their terrible experience, she made an instrument of reeds. Reeds of thirteen different lengths were bound together in the shape of a bird's tail, to make a kind of panpipe. When blown, the pipes gave a clear and very musical sound.

There were some things, however, that even Nüwa could do nothing about. When the mountain pillar fell it landed on the north-east corner of the land and for ever after this remained much lower in level than the rest. That is why all the rivers and streams in China tend to flow eastwards, pouring their waters into the great ocean that formed in the hollow east of the land. If you look at a map of China, you will see that all the major rivers still to this day flow eastwards to the sea.

Isles of the Blest

When the early humans discovered that the rivers and streams of China all flowed into the great sea in the east, they began to worry that it would one day be filled and that the water would overflow the land. If that were to happen it would bring a new disaster on mankind. However, there was no need for alarm; to the far east of the seas, no-one knows just how far, there was a great gulf. This gulf was so deep that it could fairly be called limitless and so wide that it could never be filled. Into it flowed all the waters of the sea but even when all the rivers in China were carrying their torrents of spring flood water to the sea the gulf was never completely full.

The surface of the water inside the gulf formed a second level of sea in which there were once five quite large islands, each with a mountain in the middle. These were the paradise islands, peopled by gods and immortals who lived in palaces made of gold with pillars of white jade. The birds that flew around the islands had either the whitest of feathers or the brightest, most multicoloured plumage that can be imagined. The trees where they roosted bore real pearls as well as edible fruits of every delicious flavour which gave immortality to anyone who ate them.

The inhabitants of these islands lived a happy, carefree life. The only thing that occasionally troubled them was that, marvellous as the islands were, they had one drawback. They were floating islands, not rooted to the bottom of the sea but free to wander around the great deep gulf, sometimes resting here, sometimes there, changing places with each other and generally feeling rather unstable. Tiring of this wandering existence, the immortals went to speak to the High God in Heaven, Tiandi (whose name means Emperor of the Heavens), asking that, for their safety, the islands should be secured. The god understood their problem and although even he could not root the islands in a gulf that had no bottom, he found a way of helping them. Five giant tortoises were chosen to carry the five islands on their backs and swim with them in the sea. The tortoises were extremely slow moving and steady and they could be depended upon not to upset the island immortals. Everyone was quite satisfied with the new arrangement and life continued uneventfully.

Then came a terrible disaster. A giant of no great intelligence and even less purpose decided to go fishing. He sat on a great rock at the very edge of the land and cast his long line far out over the waves, far beyond the curve where the sea meets the sky. The line was heavy as he pulled it in and as the end appeared over the horizon he saw two great tortoises floundering upside down in the water, the islands they carried on their backs quite submerged. Well pleased with his catch, the giant unceremoniously fished the tortoises out of the sea and took them home with him for a mighty meal.

The inhabitants of the two drowned islands were, of course, very shocked as their whole world literally turned upside down and their beautiful homes were destroyed. Together they made their way to Heaven to complain bitterly to the High God Tiandi. The High God listened sympathetically.
'Your situation is, of course, quite impossible,' he said at last, 'for with giants of this size in the world, the same thing could very well happen again. The only way to make sure you are all safe is for the giants to be made smaller. As for the other three islands, I can assure you that they will remain safe.'

From that time, the giants became considerably smaller and were no longer a threat to the island dwellers. As Tiandi had promised, the remaining islands continued to be safely carried on the backs of the tortoises, and were perfectly stable and secure. Their names are Penglai, Fanghu and Yingzhou and from time to time since those early days they have been heard of as the refuge of immortals and other unusual men and women who find peace there from the turmoils of the human world.

Kuafu chases the sun

One of the giants living in the dawn of time was a man named Kuafu. Kuafu was an enormous and impressive person but, like many giants, he was not terribly intelligent. He loved to watch the sun rising in the east every morning and see it fall below the horizon in the west every evening and he said to himself, 'I hate the darkness. Where is it that the sun disappears to in the west? Where does he hide himself till the next morning? If I could fix the sun in my sky I need never live in darkness.' He thought for some time. Then, 'I know. I will chase the sun and seize him so that I shall have his

light all the time, both by night and day.'

Kuafu began his pursuit of the sun on the plains of north China. Being a giant he had very long legs and in one day he covered over two thousand miles. By evening he was in sight of the place where the sun rested at night. Gleeful with the anticipation of success, he reached out his hands to seize the bright ball of fire. Then suddenly he felt a terrible thirst, a thirst such as he had never known before and could not ignore. It seemed to attack his whole body, burning him up. He turned to the nearest stream and with one draught drank it dry. It did no more to quench his thirst than a drop of water. He ran to another stream, then to another and another, but they, too, were not enough.

With his great giant steps he strode back across the land he had covered during the chase, drinking dry all the wells, streams and rivers he passed, even draining the waters of the Yellow River and the Yangtze. Still he thirsted. His only hope was to reach the sea where surely he could at last find enough water to satisfy him. Before he could reach the shore, however, he fell down in exhaustion and as the sun's last golden evening rays touched him lying there stretched out on the ground, he gave a long sigh. Summoning all his strength he flung his staff at the sun as a last gesture of anger, then closed his eyes in sleep.

Next morning when the white rays of the morning sun shone once again from the east and touched the figure of the sleeping giant he was a giant no more; in his place was a massive mountain range. To the west of the mountains was a grove of trees in the shape of a long staff and although the trees had not even been there the day before, now their leaves were green and their fruit glimmered pink and luscious among the branches. These trees had grown from the peach tree staff that Kuafu had thrown at the sun and they bore the most succulent fruit ever known, peaches that will always revive a man, will quench the most raging thirst and encourage him not to give up.

People say that the body of the giant formed the great range of mountains in the province of Shaanxi, nowadays called Mount Chiu. At the western end of the range lies a country which to this day is still called the Peach Grove.

The giant without a head

There was once a giant who had no name—but great ambitions: he wanted nothing less than to fight the High God Tiandi and steal his throne. With a round shield on his left arm and an axe in his right hand he climbed straight to Heaven, shouting his battle cry and challenging the High God to fight.

'Who dares to challenge me?' roared Tiandi angrily and, seizing his sword, he ran out to face the giant.

For days they battled, striking blow after blow, whirling round each other, pausing neither for food nor rest. As they fought they moved constantly, shifting their feet to find a better position, retreating imperceptibly down into the world of men. They fought right along the great mountain ranges of western China until they came to a mountain called Changyang. There Tiandi raised his sword high in the air and, with a mighty blow, struck the giant's head right off his shoulders, sending it rolling down the hill like a boulder. The sound of the head tumbling down the mountain was like thunder and the noise echoed and boomed through all the valleys and forests.

Amazingly, the giant's great body did not fall. For a full minute he stood there, stunned by the blow, then, in a panic, he shifted his axe to his left hand and bent down to search the ground for his head. All the nearby mountain peaks shook as his giant hand swept over them, dislodging rocks and sending landslides clattering into the valleys below. Trees were shattered, a cloud of pieces of wood, small stones and dust rose high in the air, blotting out the sunlight.

The High God Tiandi looked on from a distance, afraid that the giant would find his head, put it back on his shoulders again and renew the fight. Swiftly he took his sword and struck open the side of the mountain near where the head had finally come to rest. The great head rolled into the chasm and with a thud the mountain closed up again. With a triumphant laugh Tiandi returned to Heaven, leaving the giant standing on the mountainside, listening to the echoes of the rocks clashing together, his headless body turning from side to side trying to sense what had happened.

Still the giant with no name was undefeated. As he stood there new eyes appeared on his chest and his navel became a new mouth. Dancing a war dance that made the mountains shake once more and waving his axe defiantly, he bellowed his challenge to the skies.

'Come out and meet your challenger, High God of Heaven!'

For all we know, he stands there to this day.

The Yellow Emperor

The Yellow Emperor was an important god in ancient times. He was a very powerful figure and had many children some of whom were gods and some humans. He took a great interest in the human race and because he protected them and helped them to lead a peaceful, settled life, he was often considered to be an earthly emperor, the first to rule over China.

One of his greatest deeds was his defeat of a monster named Chiyou. Chiyou started life as quite a lowly god whose task was to be a runner for the Yellow Emperor, one who cleared the way for him when he went on a journey. Chiyou was, however, very ambitious and he planned to overthrow the Yellow Emperor and take his throne. Chiyou gathered as his followers some eighty minor gods who were discontented with the Yellow Emperor's reign. These gods were terrible to look at: they had iron heads and copper faces with four eyes, six hands and cloven feet. Their food was stones and metal and their special skill was making iron weapons of every kind—sharp lances, spears, axes and strong bows. When Chiyou had trained and organized these demon gods in Heaven, he went down to earth. There he visited the barbarian tribe of the Miao in the south of China, stirring up rebellion and discontent against the Yellow Emperor.

All this time the Yellow Emperor was living comfortably in his palace in Heaven, unaware of the scheming and plotting that was going on all around him. It was therefore a great surprise when Chiyou suddenly attacked with his fearsome army of copper-faced demons. At first the Yellow Emperor tried to reason with Chiyou, but Chiyou was too obsessed with ambition and refused to listen.

The battle began in earnest. Swords and armour clanged and clashed and the peaceful air was filled with battle cries. Chiyou was determined to win by any means and at the height of the battle he used his magic powers to surround the Yellow Emperor's army in a thick fog. The Yellow Emperor tried to muster his men and break out of the all-enveloping cloud, but it was no use. Try as they might, they simply found themselves marching in circles, while the sinister fog swirled around them.

Just when everything looked desperate, one of the Yellow Emperor's ministers who was fighting with him in the royal chariot, had an idea. 'If only we could see the stars through this cloud we could find our direction easily. Now, I wonder. What if we had something that would keep its direction like the North Star. Something that would guide us all out of the mist . . .'

The minister set to work at once with his magical powers and within minutes he had invented and made the first compass. With this marvellous new instrument the Emperor and his army easily found their way out of the fog and the battle began again as fiercely as ever.

Now the Yellow Emperor summoned another of his warriors, Yinglong (his name means Dragon Ying), a god who could make rain at will. 'Bring me a storm that will flood this rebel out of Heaven,' he commanded. But Chiyou was once again too clever for him. Before Yinglong had even started his magic, Chiyou brought a downpour of rain that stranded the Yellow Emperor's entire army. Still the Yellow Emperor was undismayed. He called one of his daughters, a goddess who was always burning hot, and as soon as she arrived the heat from her fiery body dried up the rain, leaving only small, steaming puddles which quickly evaporated. The army was saved but the Yellow Emperor's daughter had quite exhausted her powers and could no longer remain in heaven. No-one on earth wanted her either, for wherever she went she dried up the rivers, wells and fields and people drove her from village to village, a feared and hated outcast. Yinglong, the rain-maker, was also unable to

remain in Heaven, for he had been beaten by a superior force and was therefore discredited. He, too, stayed on earth, where he became king in the south. To this day the south of China is frequently wet from his rain-making.

The Yellow Emperor now seemed to be winning the war but his army was exhausted and their morale was very low. Chiyou was still a threat and the Yellow Emperor knew that he must find some way to encourage his soldiers. After much thought he decided that what he needed was a war drum louder and more powerful than anyone had ever heard before, a drum that would really put heart into his army and fear into his enemies.

In the Eastern Sea lived a monster called Kui, a strange creature rather like an ox with one foot which lived floating in the sea, keeping company with the storms, opening its great mouth to spit out fangs of lightning and roaring like the thunder itself.

'From this Kui I will make my drum,' said the Yellow Emperor and he sent his strongest warriors to capture and kill the monster. A great drum was made from its skin but though the men beat upon it with their hands, the sound was not loud enough to please the Yellow Emperor. Then he thought of the Thunder God. With hardly a moment's hesitation he commanded the Thunder God to be killed, removed his thigh bone and gave it to the principal drummer. The great drum thundered at last, the Yellow Emperor's forces marched into battle and the copper-faced demons were routed.

The war was over in Heaven but the Miao tribes on earth were still in revolt. It did not take the Yellow Emperor long to overpower them, however, and at the same time to capture Chiyou and bind him with manacles and chains. Still Chiyou refused to surrender and the Yellow Emperor had no alternative but to have him executed.

Chiyou struggled so fiercely that the manacles around his wrists were stained with his blood and after Chiyou had been killed, the Yellow Emperor threw the manacles into the wilderness. There they became maple trees and when the leaves turned bright red each year, people said the colour was the blood and anger of Chiyou.

The bird and the sea

The Sun God had a daughter whom he loved dearly, more than all his other children. One day, to amuse herself, the little girl took a boat out on the Eastern Sea. Unfortunately a storm blew up while she was quite out of sight of land and waves the size of mountains overwhelmed the boat and drowned her. The Sun God grieved for his favourite daughter but even his powerful rays could not call her back to life and he took his grief away with him to mourn in private.

The dead girl resented her early death and her soul became a small bird called Jingwei. Jingwei had a speckled head, a white beak and red claws, and she hated the sea for depriving her of her life and for robbing her father of his child. Every day she picked up a small stone or twig in her beak and, spreading her wings, flew from the land out over the Eastern Sea. Hovering over the waves she dropped her burden into the water, hoping that one day the sea would be filled with stones and twigs.

For a long time the sea took no notice of the small bird. Then one day he laughed aloud at her, showing his foaming white teeth and taunting, 'Tiny bird, tiny bird, cease your labour. Your work will never be done, not in a million years. How can you think that you can ever fill the sea up with stones and twigs?'

The bird beat her wings and cried, 'What if I drop stones and twigs for a million years, for a million times a million years, until the end of the world? I shall never stop and one day I shall fill you right up.'

'Why do you hate me so much?'

'Because you took away my young life and the lives of countless, countless others who have died from your cruelty.'

'Stupid bird,' jeered the sea again. 'You will never succeed.'

'I will, I will,' came the mournful cry of the bird as she hovered over the sea. 'One day I will succeed.'

The small bird flew back to land, only to return again, time after time, to drop her small stones and twigs into the waves. And so she continues to this day.

The cuckoo

In the ancient kingdom of Shu which we now call the province of Sichuan, there was once a king called Wang. Wang was originally a god who lived in Heaven. He came down to visit earth and there met a woman, also an immortal, who had left her home in a deep well and taken up residence in Shu. The two immortals were married and reigned together over the land.

King Wang was a benevolent ruler and was always concerned about the welfare of his people. He taught them the best way to farm the land and how to observe the seasons. The kingdom became prosperous but there was still one problem that Wang could not solve. Every year the great Yangtze river running through the kingdom overflowed its banks and destroyed vast areas of crops. Although Wang wanted to do all he could for his people, he was quite unable to control the flood water.

Then one day the corpse of a man was found floating in the Yangtze. It was obvious that this was no ordinary corpse for instead of floating downstream with the current, it floated upstream. Even more mysteriously, as soon as the people pulled it out of the river, the corpse revived. When the stranger could speak clearly, he told them that he was from Chu, several thousand miles downstream and that he had slipped and fallen into the river.

Wang soon heard of the stranger's arrival and was immediately curious to see him. When they met he was most impressed by the stranger's wisdom and knowledge, especially as he appeared to know a great deal about rivers and water control. In Wang's anxiety to find a solution to the flooding problem, he took the stranger into his court and made him an important minister.

The new minister had not been at court for long when the Yangtze flooded again. He saw at once what was causing the trouble. In that part of the country the river ran through a series of gorges which were too narrow to contain the rush of water from the hills when the snow melted in spring. The water quickly rose above the level of the banks and spread over the plateau on either side. The minister showed the people how to bore

tunnels in the mountains which allowed the water to escape from the main river channel and so the land of Shu was saved.

Wang made up his mind to cede his throne to this man who could control the water and he himself left the court and went to live quietly in the western mountains. He had only been there for a little time, however, when he heard rumours that were very harmful to his good name. According to the rumours, while the man from Chu had been busy organizing the flood control work, Wang had seduced his wife. When the husband returned and found them together, Wang, in shame, had given him the throne.

Wang never recovered from the shock of hearing these lies and deeply regretted his act of generosity. Soon, in unhappiness and frustration, he died. His spirit turned into the bird we know as the cuckoo. In Chinese its mournful cry sounds like 'Better return', and for ever after the bird has cried out Wang's regret at leaving his people.

Some people tell a different story to explain the origin of the cuckoo and its call. According to them, Wang died naturally and happily among his people. However, his love for them was so great that his spirit returned to them as the cuckoo at the beginning of every planting season. Its unusual cry was a signal to remind the people to hurry to plant their seeds and to observe the proper seasons in their farming.

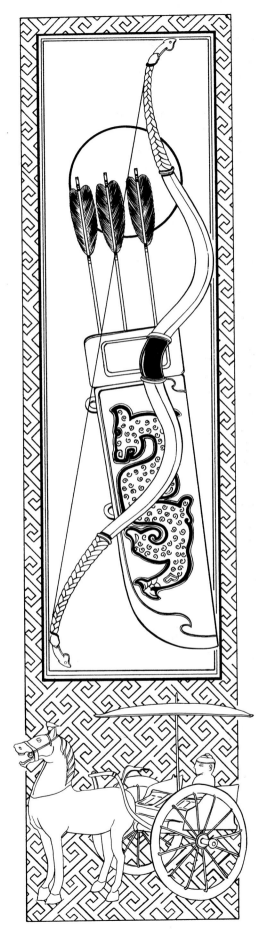

The early heroes

In the sea beyond the Eastern Ocean, at the far eastern end of the world, grew a tree called Fusang. This tree was many thousands of feet tall and about a thousand feet in girth. In its spreading branches suns roosted like birds.

In those ancient days there was not just one bright, fiery golden sun but ten. They spent their nights frolicking in the sea, bathing to renew their brightness and, later, roosting in the great Fusang tree. They took it in turns to circle the earth and shine down on the humans so that the people on earth thought there was only one sun giving them light and heat. They did not know about the other nine at the eastern end of the world who made the sea they bathed in scorching hot.

These ten suns were the children of the God of the East, Dijun, by his wife Shiho, the Goddess of the Sun. One day the ten brothers, like naughty children disobeying their parents' rule, came out into the sky all at once instead of following their usual, orderly routine. With ten suns shining all at once it became so bright and hot that everything burned up. Perhaps the suns were so pleased with all their dazzling light that they expected the people on earth to be happy also, but this was not so. The people hated them. The earth dried up, crops, flowers and trees shrivelled, even rocks and minerals seemed to melt. The blood drummed in the people's veins and they could scarcely breathe by day or night. They had little to eat and, since all the rivers dried up, very little to drink. To make matters worse, terrifying monsters emerged from forests whose greenness had been reduced to withered sticks and from the depths of the shrinking lakes and rivers.

Although the suns' father, Dijun, lived up in Heaven, he was not deaf to the pleadings of the people or to the prayers offered desperately by their ruler, the Emperor Yao. Unable to control his unruly children by reason, he decided to take drastic measures. He summoned an immortal archer whose name was Yi. Dijun gave Yi a red bow and a quiver full of white arrows and sent him down to earth.
'Do what you must,' he said, 'but do not hurt my sons more than is necessary.'

Yi obeyed. Taking with him his wife Chang'o, he went straight to the Emperor's palace where he saw for himself the terrible devastation the suns had brought and the suffering of the people, fewer and fewer

of whom came each day to beg for help.

First Yi strode to a high place and threatened the suns as they danced in the sky; he hoped that the mere sight of the magic bow and arrows would have an effect on them. However, the suns had tasted power and were in no mood to be easily frightened. They took no notice at all.

Next Yi fitted an arrow to his bow, took careful aim at one sun and loosed his arrow. A moment later a ball of fire fell heavily to the ground. Immediately the air grew a little cooler and grateful people hurried to see their fallen enemy. All they found was a giant three-footed crow lying crumpled on the ground.

Yi fitted another arrow, fired, and another ball of fire fell from the sky. At his feet another three-footed crow lay dead. Still the suns refused to obey and, as one by one Yi's arrows found their marks, the parched earth began to breathe again.

Fortunately for the earth, the Emperor realized that at least one sun must remain to provide warmth and light. Creeping up behind Yi, he counted the arrows still remaining in his quiver, then turned to count the fallen crows. Four arrows were in the quiver; six crows lay on the ground. Quickly the Emperor stole one arrow out of the quiver to make sure that at least one sun would survive. Yi was too busy to notice what was happening and continued to fire his arrows until he had no more left. One sun, pale after the overpowering brightness of the ten, still hung sadly in the sky, never again to stray from his lonely path.

The suns were gone but before the earth could return to normal life again, the monsters had to be controlled. With a fresh supply of arrows, Yi hunted them down mercilessly. On the plains he found one that the people called Great Wind. Great Wind was an enormous bird, shaped like a giant peacock with a long, spreading tail and a cruel, eagle beak. Like an eagle it would swoop down to carry off both cattle and men. Its wingspan was so great that whenever it flew, a whirlwind blew in its wake.

Yi knew that Great Wind's wings were so powerful and its flight so swift that it could easily escape before he had had the chance to shoot more than a single arrow. Sheltering on some mountain crag far away it would wait for its wounds to heal, then return to cause more havoc on the plains. To prevent this, Yi tied a strong black rope made of silk to the stem of his arrow. Taking careful aim, he shot the arrow so that it fastened right in the middle of the great bird's breast. Before the bird realized what was happening, Yi had pulled strongly on his end of the rope and dragged the monster to the ground so that he could kill it with his knife.

Yi travelled on to Lake Dongting, which lies in the central reaches of the River Yangtze. In this lake a huge water serpent had appeared as the water evaporated, capsizing fishing boats and swallowing the fishermen before they could struggle to the shore. Yi took a small boat and rowed backwards and forwards across the lake, hoping to attract the monster's attention. He did not have long to wait. The monster's ugly head appeared first, its serpent body coiling out behind it as it raced towards its prey.

Yi shot arrow after arrow into its scaly skin but the serpent was strong and eventually Yi had to fight it at close quarters from his tiny, rocking boat. At last, with a thrust of his sword, he pierced its heart. With a last thrust of its tail the serpent disappeared forever beneath the waters of the lake. A crowd of little boats put out from the shore and the fishermen escorted Yi home. Though they urged him to stay, he refused. 'While there are still monsters roaming the earth no-one is safe. I cannot rest until they are all finally destroyed,' he said.

Yi's last fight was with a giant, man-eating boar that roamed in a forest of mulberry trees. It was as big as an ox and every night it trampled the crops, carried off cattle and sometimes even attacked villagers who were foolish enough to wander outside after dark. Even this fearsome animal was no match for Yi and his magic bow and arrows. He shot it in the legs and dragged it still alive to the villagers it had terrorized.

A great feast followed at which the boar was ceremonially killed, cooked and eaten. Even the Emperor came to celebrate the death of the last monster and the beginning of a new life of peace and security. Yi was given the very best cuts of meat to carry back with him to Heaven as a thank offering to Dijun, the god who had sent the great archer to save the earth.

Chang'o and the Elixir of Immortality

When Yi returned to Heaven with his wife Chang'o, he fully expected to be thanked and praised for the part he had played in saving the earth. It was not to be. When Yi came face to face with Dijun the god frowned angrily.

'It is true that you have served men well but do not expect me to thank you for it. You have killed my sons. I cannot think of them without grieving and whenever I see you it reminds me even more vividly of what I have lost: I cannot bear to have you in my sight. You and your wife must go to live on earth among the people you served so well and never come to Heaven again.'

In vain Yi protested that he was not responsible for the unruly behaviour of the god's sun children—that he had only carried out the god's own orders. Dijun was adamant. Yi had no alternative but to take Chang'o down to earth. To add to his despair, Chang'o reacted very badly to the news of their banishment. She was even more disappointed and aggrieved than Yi himself. 'What have *I* done to deserve this?' she complained. 'I, a goddess by birth, brought up in the luxury of Heaven. Can I be blamed for my husband's actions?' And she cursed the fate that had joined her to such a husband as Yi. However, in the end she had to obey Dijun's orders and, reluctantly the two immortals gathered together all their possessions and moved their household down to earth. Yi found a mountain place to settle and there used his skill as an archer to make a living by hunting.

Life was hard for Yi. All day he roamed the mountain forests searching for game and at night he returned exhausted to a discontented wife. Chang'o refused to adapt to her new life and never stopped reproaching him.

'If you had not shot down the suns we should still be gods in Heaven,' she would say. 'Now we are banished to live on earth among men and, like men, we shall die. Just think what that means, Yi. We, who have been immortals, must go down to the shadowy Underworld and keep company with ghosts.'

Yi could only agree gloomily and wonder what, if anything, he could do about it.

One day Chang'o herself suggested a solution. 'I have heard that there is a thing called an elixir of life,' she said, 'a drug so powerful that it gives immortality to anyone who takes it. It is said that to the west, on the Mountain of Kunlun, there lives a goddess called the Queen Mother of the West, and that she collects and keeps the elixir.'

Yi, too, had heard something about this goddess and as he had no more wish than Chang'o to live and die as a human being, he agreed to seek her help.

The Queen Mother of the West may sound like a kindly old lady with white hair but she was in fact a monster goddess. She had the face of a woman but the teeth of a tiger and her long, dishevelled hair hung heavily over her ugly body, which ended in a leopard's tail. On her head she wore a jade crown shaped like growing reeds. Her servants were three-headed bluebirds who scoured the countryside for food that would please her. Never leaving her cave, she nevertheless had the power to send plagues on mankind as a punishment for misdeeds.

The Mountain of Kunlun lay to the west of China, beyond the ranges of Tibet. Other gods lived there as well as the Queen Mother and it was a formidable fortress against intruders. The mountain was surrounded first by a moat filled with water upon which nothing could float— even the lightest bird's feather sank instantly out of sight. Beyond this was a circle of flames that burned night and day with a fiery heat. No mortal had ever penetrated these two barriers but Yi still retained some of his heavenly powers and he managed to swim the water, pass through the flames and, at last, reach the cave of the Queen Mother herself.

To his relief, the goddess was sympathetic and after hearing his story she gave him a small box. 'This is the elixir of immortality,' she said. 'Guard it well for it is very precious indeed. It is made from a magic peach tree, the fruit of which confers everlasting life. This tree flowers once every three thousand years and its fruit only appears every six thousand years. Even then the harvest is small and all that I have managed to collect is in this small box. There is enough here to give both you and your wife eternal life—but you will always live in

the world of men. You would need twice as much
of the drug to give you true immortality
and godhead. Here, take it and guard it, for it is
valuable beyond price.'

Yi returned home the way he had come and
gave the elixir to his wife, repeating all that the
Queen Mother had told him.
'In a few days time,' he said, 'I will prepare a feast
and we will take the drug. Then we will be safe
from death forever.'

Feeling much happier than he had for many
months, Yi set off the next day to hunt, hoping to

find enough food to make a good feast.

At home his wife was not so contented. She still deeply resented the fact that she, who had been a goddess, should be sent down to live the life of an ordinary mortal. For her simply to avoid death was not enough: she wanted to be a goddess once again and to live among the gods in Heaven as an equal. Trustingly, Yi had told Chang'o everything, so she knew that there was enough of the drug for one person to become fully immortal. She decided to take the whole supply and, taking the box from its hiding place, she swallowed the contents all at once and sat down to wait for the drug to work.

The powerful drug took effect immediately. Chang'o felt her body floating upwards and she slowly drifted out of the window and up, up through the air.

'Perhaps I should not really fly straight up to Heaven,' she said to herself as the earth below grew smaller and smaller. 'All the gods know who I am and they will certainly blame me for taking all the elixir for myself and leaving none for my husband. Even if the whole thing was his fault in the first place.'

She looked around her. It was night and a full moon shone overhead, surrounded by flickering stars. 'I have heard that the moon is quite uninhabited,' she said. 'That will be a good place to live.'

Slowly she rose higher and higher until at last she reached the cold, silvery moon. As she expected, it was deserted except for a cassia tree and a rabbit—shapes that we can still make out on the face of the moon when it is full. There, alone, she made her home.

We do not know if Chang'o was happy or not with her immortality. It was probably a lonely life up there in the moon. According to one version of the myth the Queen Mother of the West was so angry with her for being greedy and selfish that she turned her into a frog and kept her imprisoned on the moon. But it is kinder to think of her living there in solitary glory, looking down for ever at the earth she had chosen to leave behind.

When Yi came home and found his wife and the elixir both missing, he soon guessed what had happened. With no hope of eternal life he became a bitter and disappointed man. Now among the

servants in Yi's household there was a man called Fengmeng. Fengmeng was a clever servant and Yi singled him out for special treatment, taking him as his hunting companion and even teaching him to shoot with his bow.

Fengmeng became a very good archer but, try as he might, he could never equal his master. Once when they were out hunting together they both shot at a line of flying geese. Each loosed three arrows and though all found their mark, Yi's arrows each pierced a bird's eye while Fengmeng's merely hit different parts of the birds' bodies. As the birds scattered wildly, Yi casually loosed three more arrows and again three birds fell out of the sky, each pierced through the eye. Fengmeng knew then that he could never equal Yi's skill and he turned jealously away, brooding over his own failure.

Fengmeng grew more and more jealous as the days went by and before long his respect for his master turned to hatred. At the same time Yi was becoming an increasingly difficult master to serve, demanding, short tempered and unappreciative. It was not hard for Fengmeng to work on his fellow servants' grievances and plot against Yi's life.

One fine spring day as Yi was out hunting, the servants laid an ambush. They waited in a tree beside a narrow path they knew he would use and as he passed, brought down a hard, pointed wooden stake on his head. Yi the great archer died instantly.

Though Yi's spirit went to join the ghosts of humans in the Underworld, he was not forgotten. He was honoured both for his earlier deeds and as one of the leaders of the ghost world, charged with keeping evil spirits under control so that they should do as little harm as possible to the human race he had done so much to save.

Yü controls the flood

Yao was the first human emperor to rule China and he was the wisest, most compassionate ruler that has ever existed. He himself led the simplest of lives, with no luxuries of any kind. He put all his efforts into caring for his people. Yet he was the most unfortunate of emperors. In his reign came the great drought, when ten suns shone simultaneously in the sky. Then, just as the land was recovering, a disastrous flood almost destroyed it again.

The flood came because Tiandi, the High God in Heaven, looked down upon the humans and their wicked ways and, regardless of the suffering of many innocent people, sent the God of Water to drown their fields and homes. Many of the gods felt sorry for mankind, among them a white heavenly horse by the name of Gun. Gun seemed more affected than the other gods and when he had pleaded in vain with Tiandi, he went about Heaven in great sadness.

One day he met two friends, an owl and a tortoise. Seeing him so downcast and desolate, they asked him what the matter was.
'The earth below is flooded,' Gun replied, 'and there is nothing I can do to save it.'
'To stop a flood on earth is not such a difficult task!' replied the owl. 'What you want is a precious substance called a *Shirang*. It looks like nothing more than a clod of earth but it is actually very magical indeed. If you can manage to get even a small quantity you will be able to quell any flood. The *Shirang* will swell up to enormous size as soon as it touches water and nothing can penetrate it. But of course it is carefully hidden and even guarded.'

Gun made careful enquiries and before long he managed to find out where the magic clay was kept. He stole a few handfuls, carried it carefully down to earth and in no time had built a great, impenetrable dam against the flood water. The joy and gratitude of the people was enough to recompense him for all his efforts but the High God Tiandi was not so pleased. In fact he was furiously angry and sent the Fire God to earth to kill Gun and remove the magic clay. Once more flood water covered the land.

Because Gun had not yet finished his work his spirit did not die. Instead a son grew inside him to complete his father's task. For three years the people watched over Gun's body until the son, whose name was Yü, was ready to emerge. Once again the High God Tiandi was angry and he sent a god to kill this new threat to his plans. The god struck at Gun's body with a sword—but instead of killing the child he released him and, in the shape of a mighty dragon, Yü entered the world.

The fierce appearance of the dragon and the determination that had shaped him softened Tiandi's heart and he agreed to allow him to recall the flood.

Yü's task was not an easy one, for the Water God, Gonggong, who had been given the freedom of the land, was not willing to be recalled without a fight and he ignored all Yü's commands. Yü fought and defeated him. Then he gave all the people pieces of the magic clay to build another great dam and hold the waters back. He knew, however, that this was not a permanent solution and he next set the people to work digging a path for the water so that it could flow away harmlessly into the sea. Resuming his dragon shape, he ploughed a furrow with his tail and showed the people how to dig it into deep channels. The flood water that flowed away through these channels to the sea formed the great rivers of China.

Yü was thirty years old before he had time to pause in his work and think about marriage. Not knowing how to choose a wife, he waited for a sign, which soon came in the shape of a white fox with nine tails. The fox led him to a girl who lived on nearby Mount Tu where the marriage contract was made and Yü and his new wife began to live happily together.

Yü's wife, however, never knew that her husband was a god and some months later when she was expecting her first child her ignorance caused a tragic accident. Yü was still busy controlling water and one day he changed himself into a bear in order to dig a tunnel for water to run through a hill. His wife saw him in his bear form and ran away in terror. When he followed her to explain she only ran faster and faster until at last she dropped down exhausted and was turned into a stone. Horrified, Yü rushed up to the stone and knocking on it called out loudly: 'Give me my son!' The stone burst open and Yü's son Chi was born.

With his son to help him Yü continued his task of taming the waters and killing the monsters that had appeared during the time of the flood. In his old age he was elected emperor to succeed Yao's heir and ruled over the land wisely until his death.

The child abandoned on the ice

During the reign of Yao the land of China gradually recovered from its droughts and floods and the people began to live normal lives. It was at this time that one of the founders of the Chinese way of life, Houji, was born.

Houji's mother's name was Jiangyuan but no-one knew who his father was. One day Jiangyuan was returning home along the path beside the river when she saw a line of giant footprints which both frightened and intrigued her. She fitted her own small feet into the first print and walked a little way along, jumping from print to print. Little did she know that by treading in these footprints she had conceived a child but in time the boy Houji was born.

As Houji had no father, his mother's family were afraid of a scandal and as soon as the child was born they snatched him from Jiangyuan's arms and threw him in a narrow lane where cattle and sheep were driven regularly—expecting that in no time he would be trampled to death. Instead the cattle and sheep not only walked carefully round him, they also suckled him with their milk so that he thrived. When the family saw this they took him back again and abandoned him in a deep forest. Again they were unsuccessful. Woodmen coming to cut wood found the child and brought him back, thinking he had been lost accidentally. Finally, in desperation, they exposed him on the cold ice of a frozen river, but the birds flew down and covered him with their wings to keep him warm.

Certain now that this was no ordinary child, the family rescued him and restored him to his mother.

Houji was an extraordinary child. While he was still very young he learned to pick and sort wild grain and edible beans of every variety. He plucked them from the wilderness and cultivated them near his home so that they grew large and succulent and fed the people well. He also began to make simple agricultural implements such as hoes. Eventually the emperor himself heard of Houji's work and invited him to become a minister of the state so that he could spread his knowledge of grains and agriculture to all the people of China.

Even after Houji's death he continued to improve the crops. The land where he was buried became exceptionally fertile and yielded the grains he had domesticated in greater quantities than anywhere else in China.

Shun the wise emperor

While Houji was growing up and bringing settled agriculture to China, another boy, Shun, was born. Not long after Shun was born his mother died and his father, who was blind, married again. From this marriage were born a boy called Shiang and a girl called Shi.

Shun's was not a happy family. The blind father was blind not only in his eyes but in his heart and head as well for he doted on his second wife and her children and totally ignored his eldest son. Shun's stepmother, a mean and greedy woman, hated him and did her best to make life difficult for him. So did her son Shiang, whose face was disfigured with a gigantic nose. The only person who had any regard for him at all was his half-sister Shi.

Life became more and more unbearable for Shun in his father's house and in the end he ran away from home. Though Shun's relations did not appreciate him, he had an extraordinary effect on all the other people he met: wherever he went he was welcomed by the people and under his influence they forgot their quarrels and started to work together more peacefully. The Emperor Yao soon came to hear of this unusual man and summoned him to court. Like everyone else he was very impressed by Shun. In fact he was so pleased with him that he decided that one day Shun should inherit his kingdom. To make the inheritance easier, he gave Shun his two daughters in marriage.

When Shun's family heard about his good fortune they were full of envy and hated him more than ever. The most envious of them all was his brother Shiang, for he coveted his beautiful sisters-in-law. Together with the old, blind father, he plotted to have Shun killed.

Shiang came one day to the house where Shun was living and asked him to help repair the family barn. Of course Shun agreed, suspecting nothing. Shun's wives, however, were not so trusting and, fearing for his safety, they pleaded with him not to go. Unable to persuade him of the danger, they gave him a many-coloured coat on which was painted a large bird.
'Wear this all the time you are with your family,'

they said. 'Then you will come to no harm, whatever they are plotting.'

Shun clambered up a high ladder to inspect the roof of the barn and just as he reached the ridge and was about to shout down that he could find nothing wrong, Shiang removed the ladder, leaving him stranded. To Shun's horror he saw that Shiang and his father had set light to the barn and that flames were leaping towards him as its dry wood crackled and burned.
'Help me, someone,' cried Shun—but the small figures far below merely stood back to watch. Then suddenly the many-coloured coat with its bird painting came to life, spread strong, feathered wings and flew off into the sky, carrying Shun to safety.

A few weeks later Shun's wicked stepbrother tried again. He called at the court, full of soft words and apologies and this time asked for help in cleaning out the bottom of the well. Again, Shun's wives tried to persuade him not to go and again, when he refused to listen to them, they gave him a piece of clothing. This time it was a coat painted with the picture of a dragon.

'Wear this under your ordinary clothes,' they advised him, 'and only reveal the pattern if you are in extreme danger.'

Shun arrived at his father's house and although the family looked at him very closely they did not see any unusual clothing.

'Now we shall succeed,' they whispered.

The well was deep and Shiang lowered Shun down, tied to a long rope. When he was about half-way down there was a sudden jerk on the rope and Shun found himself falling faster and faster with stones rattling past him. His evil brother had cut the rope and, to make quite sure Shun could not escape, was hurtling rocks after him into the well.

Shun dodged the stones and just before he reached the water he managed to strip off his outer coat and reveal the dragon-patterned one he wore underneath. Immediately, Shun himself became a dragon, slipped into the water and swam along the underground stream that supplied the well until he reached safety above ground at another place.

Shiang was still determined to kill Shun and after a great deal of thought he decided on a new plot. He invited Shun to a family feast, intending that Shun should get thoroughly drunk on specially prepared wine. Then, while he slept heavily, Shiang would be able to kill him. Fortunately Shun's sister Shi warned him of the plot and once again he went to his wives for help. 'Take this powder,' they told him, 'dissolve it in your bath before you go to the feast and wash yourself carefully in it.'

The feast began. Pretending to treat him with great respect, the family brought dish after dish of food and plied him with cup after cup of wine. But however much wine he drank he did not become in the least drunk. Finally he walked away from the table leaving everyone else completely intoxicated.

The Emperor Yao was very satisfied with his son-in-law's character and behaviour and he made up his mind to give him the throne at once so that Yao himself could enjoy a more carefree old age. There was just one more test he must undergo to prove himself worthy. This was a test of courage.

Yao sent Shun into a deep mountain forest. In this dark, sinister place, thunderstorms never ceased, lightning flickered dangerously among the close-growing trees and torrential rain caused unpredictable floods and avalanches. Shadowy monsters lurked among the dark trunks, waiting to attack any living creature that dared to enter their domain. Shun did not falter but walked through it all calmly, brushing the clutching undergrowth aside as if it were grass and taking no notice at all of the threatening monsters. Shun had now passed this final test and in due course he was proclaimed emperor.

The new emperor did not forget his family although they had treated him so badly. He gave his father a pension and, seeing that he regretted his former wickedness, forgave him everything. He forgave his long-nosed brother, too, but sent him to govern a far off southern colony of the kingdom, where he could not be tempted by envious thoughts.

Shun ruled for many long years and was an old man when he died travelling through the southern part of his kingdom. When they heard the news of his death, his wives set out to attend his funeral, weeping as they went. As they came to southern China, they passed through a dense grove of bamboos and their tears left dark splashes on the growing canes. Even today you can see a kind of mottled bamboo growing in the south, bearing the marks of their tears.

The two wives never reached their husband's grave. When they reached the River Shiang they tried to cross in a small boat but a storm rose and they were drowned. The gods took pity on them and made their spirits into the guardian goddesses of the River Shiang.

One day, some months after Shun had been ceremonially buried, a dark-skinned man was seen making sacrifices at his tomb. It was the brother Shiang, tanned from the tropical sun and almost unrecognizable except for his giant nose. As the people watched, they were amazed to see him turn into an elephant and then plod off to work ploughing the fields nearby, which belonged to the grave. The gods had decided he must expiate the wickedness he had shown towards Shun while he was alive and, because of his long nose, had chosen an elephant as the most suitable animal.

When gods and men mingled

In the ancient kingdom of Shu, which we now call Sichuan, there was once a ruler called Li Bing. The upper reaches of the Yangtze flowed through Shu, and the god of this part of the river was cruel and often flooded the land. Each year the river god demanded of the people of Shu that they give him two of their maidens. The people were afraid, as they knew that without the maidens the river god would flood the land. So each year they drew lots to decide which family had to provide the maidens and the treasures for their dowry. Then the two girls were put on a small raft and towed to the middle of the river, where they were left to sink. The girls drowned and the treasure sank, but though the people grieved, they did not dare do otherwise.

When Li Bing became ruler of Shu, he was determined to end the river god's tyranny. 'This year I shall give the tribute to the river god,' Li Bing said to his people. 'I shall provide the girls from my own family and the treasures from my own purse.'

When the time came, Li Bing had two of his daughters dressed in bright clothes and covered the sacrificial altars beside the river with food, wine and incense. Musicians were ordered to play, and before the image of the river god Li Bing poured out a cup of wine. He placed the full cup on the altar, saying 'I am happy to be the one to offer the sacrifice this year and trust that my lord will honour me by drinking a cup of wine.' Li Bing drank a cup himself, but the god's wine remained untouched.

'You insult me! cried Li Bing in a rage. 'How dare you not accept my wine! I shall not rest until this insult is avenged!' At this he drew out a gleaming sword and quickly disappeared from sight.

The music stopped and the people stood frightened and bewildered. Suddenly they saw the river heaving and swelling, and gradually there rose out of it a huge grey ox battling with a giant sea serpent. Still fighting, they sank again beneath the waves. Then out of the water came Li Bing, panting and bathed in sweat.

'I need your help,' he said to the crowds on the river bank. 'The river god almost defeated me, but now that he has stopped to rest I must gather my forces.' Selecting several scores of the best archers amongst his people, he armed them with strong bows and arrows and addressed them. 'Just now I assumed the form of an ox to fight the river god while he assumed the form of a serpent. Now he is certain to choose the form of an ox as well. When he does, you must shoot him down. So that you can distinguish between us, I shall tie this white silk band around my body.' Then Li Bing plunged back into the river.

The wind rose, the water heaved, and out of the waves appeared two huge oxen, fighting for their lives, clashing their horns and striking out viciously with their hooves. One of the oxen was wearing a white band around its body and, taking careful aim, the archers shot the other ox.

The ox heaved and rose in the water with blood streaming from scores of arrow wounds, turning the river red. As the ox struggled for life it suddenly changed back into the form of a giant sea serpent and in this form it floated on the red waves, half-alive and half-dead. Li Bing jumped unharmed on to the river bank to the relief and great joy of all his people. Yet he was still afraid that the river god might escape and to make certain this would never happen, he had the sea serpent seized and bound with heavy chains.

When this had been done, the people of Shu dug great tunnels and pools beneath the mountains, into which the flood waters of the river could flow and be stored. It was here that they kept the sea serpent chained up, and in later centuries these pools became known as the 'Chained Serpent Pools'. Never again did the people of Shu have to give up their daughters to the river god.

Panhu, the marvellous dog

At the court of a small Chinese kingdom there was once a queen who had the most extraordinary large ears. One day she suddenly developed earache and, much to her distress, this lasted continuously for three whole years. All kinds of doctors tried all kinds of remedies, but none was successful. Then one day a small golden worm jumped out of one of the queen's ears, and as soon as it did so, the earache stopped.

The queen was intrigued by the worm and she decided to keep it and feed it herself. She placed it inside a gourd and covered this with a plate. When

she looked into the gourd some while later, she discovered that the worm had turned into a small dog with the most beautiful fur. Because he had been reared in a gourd under a plate, the queen named the dog 'Plate-gourd', which in Chinese

was Panhu. The dog soon grew so big that on his hind legs he was taller than a man and he became a great favourite of the king, who always kept him by his side.

At that time the king was at war with a neighbouring kingdom and the battle was not going well. In fact enemy soldiers had laid siege to the king's palace. The king called his counsellors together and told them, 'If anyone can bring me the head of my enemy, I shall gladly give him the hand of my daughter, the princess, in marriage.' The counsellors all looked at each other, but they knew of the enemy king's great strength, and not one of them offered to take up the challenge.

That very day Panhu the dog disappeared and no-one in the palace could find him. They did not know that he had gone to the neighbouring kingdom and found his way into the presence of the enemy king. The king regarded the dog's appearance as a good omen and said to his courtiers, 'The seige will soon be over—even my enemy's favourite dog has deserted him!' And with this he called for a great feast to be prepared to celebrate his forthcoming victory.

At the feast the wine flowed like water, and before long the king, his courtiers and even the guards were all sound asleep. When he saw this, Panhu leaped up and bit off the king's head with one snap of his teeth. When the guards awoke they were horrified to see their king's headless body, and in their fear and confusion they ordered the seige to be ended.

When Panhu returned to the palace with the enemy king's head, everyone rejoiced and made a great fuss of him. But though they set the best meats before him, Panhu went off into a corner and sulked. The king remembered his promise and went up to Panhu.
'Will you not enjoy the feast and be my favourite again?' he asked. 'Surely you don't think that I could let you marry the princess. After all, you are only a dog and there can be no marriage between an animal and a woman.'

To everyone's surprise the dog opened his mouth and replied:
'If that is all you are concerned about, please do as I ask. Place me beneath a golden bell and let no-one look at me for seven days and seven nights. Then I can become a man.'

The king did as Panhu asked and put him under a large golden bell. For five days no-one went near or touched the bell, but on the sixth day the princess, anxious that Panhu might starve to death, went to the bell and peeped beneath it.

She saw that Panhu the dog had almost turned into a man and was completely human except for his head. Now, because she had lifted the golden bell and broken the spell, Panhu could not change his dog's head into that of a man but nevertheless he came out and dressed himself in men's clothes. The princess put on a furry hat to make her look like a dog, and she and Panhu were married.

After the wedding they left the palace and went away to lead a simple life. Panhu supported them by hunting and his wife did not complain at having to work hard. They had many sons and a daughter, and their children had families of their own until eventually there was a large clan of people who could claim Panhu as their ancestor.

The crane maiden

In those ancient days when gods and men mingled, the daughters of gods used to come down to earth, and occasionally these Heavenly Maidens would marry mortal men.

There was once a peasant by the name of Tian Kunlun, who was still a bachelor. Not far from his home there was a pool of very clear water, as deep and pure as green jade and shaded by beautiful trees. One day as he was passing by, Tian saw three beautiful young women bathing in the pool. This made him curious and he crept closer to the pool so that he could see better. As he did so, the three young women turned into white cranes and came skimming out of the water. Two of the cranes plucked up their bundles of clothes from beside the pool and flew off into the sky. But the third crane was not quite so quick and Tian reached her bundle of clothes first. The white crane fluttered around him and then went back to the pool, where once again she took the form of a beautiful young woman. She begged Tian to give her back her clothes.
'I'll give you your clothes if you will tell me who you are,' said Tian.

'I am one of the daughters of the High God,' the girl replied. 'My father gave us these clothes so that we may come and go freely in Heaven and on earth. We were just bathing in the pool and did not see you. My sisters have gone back to Heaven and I cannot follow them without my clothes. So please give them back to me. If you do, I shall willingly be your wife.'

Tian was delighted at this, but he thought that if he returned her clothes she might fly away like her sisters, never to be seen again.
'I would like nothing more in the whole world than to have you as my wife,' he said to the girl. 'I shall give you my clothes so that you can come out of the pool and return home with me. I cannot give you your own clothes in case you fly off and leave me.'

The girl was unhappy at this, but she realized that there was no other way, and so she agreed. Tian took off his outer garments and gave them to the girl who dressed herself and came out of the pool.

Tian and the girl went to his mother's house. She was delighted to have such a beautiful

daughter-in-law and immediately prepared a feast, inviting all their friends and neighbours to join in the celebration. After the wedding, Tian and his wife lived happily together and before long they had a son whom they named Tian Zhang.

Some years after the birth of his son, Tian was called away to serve as a warrior a long way from his home. Before he went away, he took his mother aside and showed her his wife's heavenly clothes, which he had kept hidden. He told his mother not to let his wife find them in case she should put them on and fly off to Heaven. Together they made a hiding place amongst his mother's boxes, and Tian went away. When he was gone, the crane maiden asked her mother-in-law every day if she knew where her heavenly clothes were, begging her for just a glimpse of them.
'If you will allow me just one look at my clothes, I shall be happy,' she said.

At this the old woman took pity on her daughter-in-law and fetched the heavenly clothes from their hiding place. The crane maiden wept to

see her clothes and took them in her arms. Before the old woman could stop her, she had put the clothes on, and in an instant had flown out of the window. The old woman rushed to the window, but her daughter-in-law was already just a small speck far away in the sky.

When Tian returned, he and his mother wept but there was nothing they could do to bring the crane maiden back. The little boy Zhang longed for his mother and searched the fields for her, weeping and calling. His cries were heard by a wise old man, who knew the cause of his tears and also knew that his mother would not have forgotten her son. 'Go to the pool near your home,' he told Zhang, 'and wait for three beautiful women dressed in white silk. Two of the women will look at you curiously, but the third one will pretend not to see you. That woman will be your mother.' Zhang did as the old man told him and went to the pool to wait.

Meanwhile the crane maiden was very unhappy in Heaven. She had thought she would be happy to be back with her heavenly family, but everything reminded her of the little son she had left behind on earth and she wept all day long. Her sisters laughed at her for being so silly, but they felt sorry for her, too, and promised that they would all go down to earth to see that her child was all right.

When the three sisters arrived at the pool where they had once bathed, Zhang was already waiting as the wise old man had told him. He saw the three women in white and went straight up to them. Two of them looked at him and smiled, saying, 'Sister, sister, here is your son'. But the third woman looked down and pretended not to see him. When he saw this, Zhang ran to her, calling 'Mother, mother!' She could not help taking him in her arms and crying tears of joy. They hugged each other for a long time, till one of the two sisters said, 'We must go back now. If you cannot bear to be parted, we had better take your son back with us to Heaven.'

Between them they lifted the little boy and flew off with him to the house of the High God. The High God was delighted with his grandson and took him into his care, giving him books and sharing with him all his knowledge. The child learned quickly and after four or five days the High God gave him eight books to take back to earth, saying, 'It is time for you to go. Take these books and study them well, for you will derive great benefit from them.'

Zhang left his mother and went back to earth with his grandfather's books. Although he had been in Heaven for only four or five days, on earth he had been away for about twenty years. His grandmother was dead and he could not find his father but his new-found knowledge made him independent and he reached a high position at the imperial court. Whenever the emperor asked for his advice, Zhang would consult his heavenly books and what he said always proved to be right. And in this way he became famous.

The herd boy and the weaving girl

When the world was new and people first lived on earth, crops were hard to raise and there was never enough food for everyone. Seeing this, the High God sent the Ox Star down to earth as a messenger, to tell people to eat only one meal every three days, with an occasional extra snack. Unfortunately the ox was not very intelligent and he told people to eat three meals every day, with an occasional snack as well. When the High God realized that the ox had delivered his message wrongly and that now there would be even less food to go round, he was enraged.

'As you have given people the wrong advice,' he told the ox, 'you had better go down to earth and help them put things right. You will become the people's servant, helping them to plough the soil and raise enough crops for their three meals a day, and their occasional extra snack!' The ox went sadly down to earth, and he and his descendants have been men's servant's since that day. We do not know whether the Ox Star himself had to stay on earth for ever, but he was almost certainly the means by which the herd boy met the weaving girl, another of the Heavenly Maidens.

The herd boy was a young man who was liked by everyone for his hard work and honesty. When his parents died his two older brothers decided to divide up the property and go their

separate ways. As they were older and more cunning, the two brothers succeeded in claiming the best land and the best animals, leaving the herd boy with nothing but an old ox and the poorest piece of land. He led the ox to his land, built a rough shelter, and together they worked hard and managed to make a modest living. Being an honest, industrious young man, the herd boy never resented or tried to cheat anyone.

One evening, exhausted from his labours in the fields, he sat beside the ox feeling lonely and sad. For though his hard work had brought him a reasonable life, he had no-one to share it with apart from the ox. Then suddenly the ox spoke: 'Please don't be so sad, master, for I can help you.'

The herd boy was astonished to hear the ox speak. 'Who are you, and how can you help me?' he asked.

'I am the Ox Star, and I really belong in Heaven,' replied the ox. 'I was sent here to work hard as a punishment. But you have been a very good master to me, and so I will help you to find a wife who will make you happy. Not far away from here there is a clear pool shaded by trees and plants. Go there tomorrow and wait for the Heavenly Maidens to come and bathe in the pool. Whilst they are bathing, steal one of the girl's clothes, so that she will not be able to fly up to Heaven. Then she will be your wife.'

The herd boy did as the ox said and waited beside the clear pool. Soon a crowd of beautiful Heavenly Maidens came down from the sky, shed their bright clothes like plumages and left them on the bank before stepping into the water. The herd boy waited and, as they came out of the water again, he sprang from his hiding place and seized one of the piles of clothes. The girls were startled and, snatching their clothes, they flew off into the sky. Only one girl was left and the herd boy came to the edge of the pool and spoke to her gently, begging her to be his wife. His soft words persuaded the girl and she agreed. Taking off his outer garments, the herd boy wrapped them round the girl and took her home.

When the Heavenly Maiden and the herd boy were married, she told him that she was the weaving girl from Heaven. She was indeed the Goddess of Weaving and her skill with all kinds of cloth stood them in good stead. Before long the income from her weaving gave them an easy, comfortable life. They were very happy together, and the weaving girl gave birth to a son and a daughter. But the gods regretted the loss of their Weaving Goddess and were anxious to have her back again in Heaven. When her grandfather, the High God, discovered that she was living with the herd boy, he thought that she was far too good for him and sent his guards down to earth to bring her back to Heaven by force.

The weaving girl's husband and children were helpless against the guards, and they watched weeping as she disappeared into the sky. Suddenly there was a bellow from the stall: 'Herd boy,' said the ox, 'I will do you one last act of kindness. I shall die here before returning to Heaven. As soon as I am dead, take off my hide and put it round you. Then you will find your wife.' When he had finished speaking, the ox dropped down dead. The herd boy was sad to lose his dear friend and adviser, but he did as the ox had said. He wrapped the ox hide round him and put a carrying pole across his shoulders, with a basket at each end. Then he put his son in one basket and his daughter in the other and, as the little girl was smaller than her brother, he also put a ladle in her basket so that it would balance. When this was done, he took his staff, left his house and found that he flew up into the sky just as his wife had done. It was not long before he could make out the figure of the weaving girl far away in the distance.

The High God was very pleased to see the weaving girl return, but he was horrified when he saw her husband following close behind. So he stretched out his hand and drew a line across the sky. This line became the Milky Way and formed a wide river which the herd boy could not cross. He stopped before it and gazed at it helplessly, till his little daughter said, 'Father, we can scoop the water out of the river with our ladle. Then we shall be able to cross.' The herd boy set to work at once, and the children helped by scooping out the water with their hands. But hard though they tried, they could not empty the river.

When the gods saw that the herd boy and his children did not give up, they were deeply moved. The High God decided that the herd boy could visit his wife once every year. He decreed that on the seventh day of the seventh month each year, all the magpies on earth would fly up into the sky and form a bridge across the water so that the herd boy could cross. When the weaving girl met her husband, she was so happy that she would sometimes cry and on that night the earth would receive a gentle shower of rain. Then all the mothers on earth would say to their children, 'Poor weaving girl, she is crying again.'

The herd boy and the weaving girl were in the sky for so long that finally they turned into stars. When we look up at the sky, we see a bright star on one side of the Milky Way in the constellation of Vespa: this is the weaving girl. On the other side we see another bright star (Aquila) with two small stars beside it: this is the herd boy and the two children. There are three other stars near the weaving girl and it is said that these are the crooked staff for herding cattle which the herd boy threw to his wife. Near the herd boy are four more small stars which people say are the shuttle which the weaving girl threw to her husband. It is said that during the long days and nights they are apart, the couple hang messages on the staff and shuttle and throw them across the river. Looking at these distant stars, all parted lovers remember the herd boy and the weaving girl and gain courage from their example of faithfulness.

The silkworm

A man who lived with his wife and daughter was called far away to the Chinese border to serve in the wars. The man was very unhappy at having to leave his family, but his wife and daughter did their best to carry on with their lives as normal. Nevertheless, they were lonely without the father, and the young girl took great comfort from looking after the family's horse. She would groom and feed the horse every day, making sure it was happy and at the same time thinking of her father. One day, as she was grooming the horse in the stable, she said dreamily, 'If only you could run to the border and bring my father home from the war. If anyone could do that, I would gladly marry him and serve him. Even if it were you.'

As soon as the horse heard this, he whinnied and reared up on his hind legs, tearing the rope that secured him to the stable. Before the young girl could do anything, the horse had galloped out into the courtyard and away. He made for the Chinese border and after a few days managed to find the father. The man was astonished to see the horse and hoped that he had brought a message from his family. But when he saw that there was no message, he became worried that something had happened to his family while he was away. The horse seemed to be inviting him to ride, so he jumped on the horse's back and, carefully avoiding the guards, galloped off home.

His wife and daughter were overjoyed to see him home again, but he was puzzled to find nothing wrong except that they had missed him so much. Finally he decided that the horse must have been intelligent enough to see how distressed his mistress was. In thanks he found all the best hay and oats to feed to the horse and did everything he could to make him happy. However, the horse refused to eat and stayed in a corner of the stable, looking very unhappy. He only became lively when the daughter of the house came near, and then he would neigh, rear up and become almost uncontrollable. The young girl avoided the stable as much as possible and looked guilty whenever the horse saw her.

Her father saw all this and was extremely puzzled. One day he took his daughter aside and asked her if she could explain the horse's strange behaviour. At first she said that she did not understand either, but in the end she admitted that she had promised to marry the horse if he brought her father home from war. At this her father became very angry and spoke to her harshly: 'It was immodest of you even to think of such an idea! From now on I forbid you to leave the house!'

Although the man was very fond of the horse, he felt that he could not allow him to marry his daughter; and although the girl stayed indoors, the horse continued to behave in a strange fashion. In the end the man could bear it no longer and, taking a bow and arrow, he went to the stable and shot the horse. Thinking he had solved a difficult problem, he took the horse's skin, put it in the sun in the courtyard and thought no more

about it. His daughter was relieved to hear that the horse was dead and she went running happily out into the sunshine of the courtyard. As she went past the horse's skin, a great gust of wind came from nowhere and wrapped the skin around the girl's shoulders. It blew like a whirlwind right out of the courtyard and carried the girl far away into the wilderness.

The man and his wife were horrified to see what had happened and he quickly ran after the whirlwind. He followed it through the wilderness for days and eventually the whirlwind seemed to get smaller and smaller until it almost disappeared altogether. It finally came to rest in a mulberry tree and the father rushed up to it. On searching

the tree, he found a small worm crawling along a mulberry leaf and realized that this was all that was left of his daughter.

Sadly, he took the worm home and fed it every day with mulberry leaves. In time he noticed that the worm made a fine, strong, thread and when it produced more worms he found that he and his wife could weave the fine thread into a most wonderful cloth. The cloth was soft and beautiful to the touch, and they called it silk. Eventually as there were more and more worms, the people of China produced large amounts of silk for which they became famous. And in later centuries the silk makers worshipped the silkworm maiden who had presented this gift to men.

The Chinese dragons

The dragon is the most striking beast in Chinese mythology, and he appears very frequently in the ancient stories. The Chinese dragon, *long*, was very different from European dragons. He breathed not fire but clouds and has been described as having the head of a camel, the horns of a stag, the eyes of a demon, the ears of a cow, the neck of a snake, the belly of a clam, the scales of a carp, the claws of an eagle and the paws of a tiger. Very often, however, he appeared in human form. His element was water and he controlled rainfall as well as the water in rivers, lakes and streams. Unlike the dragon of European mythology, he was usually a well-meaning creature, although sometimes given to fits of rage when he caused havoc with storms and floods. Each sea, river or lake had its guardian dragon, often of kingly status, living in a crystal underwater palace surrounded by priceless treasures. Though he guarded his treasure jealously from thieves, he occasionally gave a share to a mortal who had pleased him in some way. As guardian spirits dragons belonged to the race of immortals and mixed freely with gods and goddesses, who sometimes used them as mounts as they rode about the sky.

The dragon was also an important and powerful symbol. The Chinese believed that there was a male principle *(yang)* and a female *(yin)* in all things in the universe. The sun, for example was male, the moon female. Dragons represented the male principle and were used as a symbol of all things male. In the same way the phoenix, *feng*, was used as a symbol of all things female. The dragon was also the symbol of the Emperor of China, who was said to sit on the dragon throne, often accompanied by a phoenix symbolizing the Empress. The imperial dragon is shown with five claws instead of the usual four, to distinguish him from all lesser beasts.

Dragon images were familiar to Chinese people in ordinary life, and two popular festivals featured the dragon. The fifteenth day of the first month in the lunar calendar, falling at the end of February by our reckoning, was a holiday to mark the end of the Chinese New Year celebrations and the coming of spring. On this day the dragon dance was performed in public. A number of men each held up on a stick a lantern which was made to look like the segment of a dragon. They all stood in a line, with the first lantern painted to look like a dragon's head and those behind smaller and smaller until the last looked like a tail. To perform the dance, the men wore black clothes and turned and moved in line so that in the dark their lanterns looked like a brightly lit dragon writhing along. Another dancer would hold a separate lantern, painted to look like a red ball. This represented a pearl, and the line of dancers would move in such a way that the dragon seemed to be chasing after the pearl. People generally regarded this dance as a holiday spectacle, but its origin was probably an ancient religious ritual symbolizing the rousing of the earth in preparation for the sowing season.

The second popular event was the dragon boat festival, which was also both a holiday and a ritual and which was held at the beginning of summer on the fifth day of the fifth month in the lunar calendar, corresponding to some time around the middle of June. Boats were built with dragon-shaped prows, and teams of men would compete against each other in rowing races, with a grand prize for the winning boat. This is thought to have been a rain-making festival, as summer rain was important for the rice crop. But another story has arisen to explain the origin of the dragon boat festival.

In about the fourth century BC there was a minister in the kingdom of Chu by the name of Chü Yüan. He was an honourable man and was much loved by the people, but his king was foolish enough not to heed his advice and finally he had the minister banished. Chü Yüan wandered about the countryside writing poems which have survived to this day but in the end his banishment caused him to despair and he drowned himself. After his death, he appeared to those he had loved in a dream, telling them to give sacrifices to his spirit by throwing food wrapped in bamboo leaves into the river, and he added that they should scare away demons and ghosts with racing boats which had dragon-shaped prows. His friends did as he said, and in later centuries people continued to wrap food in bamboo leaves before steaming it as a mark of remembrance to the dead minister. And the dragon boat races are still held.

It is sometimes said that the Chinese dragon kings can be identified with the Indian serpent demons, stories of which travelled to China with Buddhist missionaries. Whilst some of the dragon stories in Chinese mythology were probably influenced by Indian myths, the well-meaning, guarding aspect of the Chinese dragons make them very different and quite unique.

Gaoliang bridge

In Chinese popular superstition dragons were thought to be responsible for invisible lines that ran across the earth, rather like the ley lines of ancient Britain. These dragon lines were considered to be the earth's veins, through which natural forces flowed, and if they were obstructed disasters would befall that particular area. These ideas formed part of the theories upon which the art of geomancy was based, geomancy being a form of divination that sought to read the earth's surface in much the same way as a fortune-teller might read your palm. In reality the dragon lines often followed natural geological features, running along mountains, ridges and rivers. But people believed very strongly that the lines should not be interfered with, otherwise a dragon's anger might be aroused. The following story tells of how a dragon was indeed offended by people building on his land and how, in spite of this and with a little supernatural help, the people triumphed in the end.

Centuries ago the area which is now the city of Peking was a very dismal place, the site of the salt marshes of Youzhou. The people of the area lived along the edges of the marsh or up in the nearby hills, and the marsh itself was inhabited by a dragon and his family. Because several dragon lines crossed at this point, following the path of rivers along the foothills, the dragon reigned supreme. It so happened, however, that the Emperor of Ming had chosen this place for the site of his new capital, and he was supported in this by a powerful Taoist god called Nocha. This god was a mighty warrior with eight arms, but he would often appear in the form of a small boy dressed in a pair of red trousers. He was aware that the dragon lived here and had encouraged the architect and builders to place the city right over the dragon's lair. The god and the dragon were

determined to do battle for possession of the site.

As the building work progressed and walls and towers began to rise into the sky, the dragon could see his kingdom being taken away from him. He was determined not to allow this and decided that he would prevent the city from ever being inhabited. He appeared before the emperor in a dream, taking the form of a harmless old man who with his wife was pushing a small handcart containing two large jars of water. He asked the emperor's permission to take the jars out of the city, which the emperor readily gave. The emperor did not know that he was being cheated, for in fact the jars in the dream contained all the water in the new city of Peking. As soon as he awoke from his dream, the emperor heard terrible cries from all parts of the half-built city; all the springs and wells had suddenly dried up and there was not a drop of water left in the city.

Although the god Nocha had been too late to prevent the dragon from emptying the city of all its water, he quickly thought of a way to get it back. He sent a dream to the chief architect, Liu Bowen, who on waking was able to react swiftly to the terrible news about the water. First he sent messengers to all the city gates to find out who had left the city that day, and then he called together the emperor's army in order to find a volunteer for a very dangerous task. The messengers soon returned and there was news from the west gate that an old man and his wife had left the city at dawn pushing a handcart containing two heavy water jars. So Liu Bowen knew that the dragon had left by the west gate. He also knew that a hundred leagues away, in a straight line across the hills, was the sea. If the dragon were to succeed in emptying the water jars into the sea, there would be no way of getting any more water to the springs of Peking.

Liu Bowen addressed the assembled army, explaining the situation and asking for a brave soldier to ride after the dragon and stop him from pouring all the water into the sea. Once the soldier had caught up with the dragon, he was to pierce the water jars with his lance and return to the city without looking back. It would be a dangerous mission, as the dragon might realize what the soldier intended. When they heard this, the soldiers all looked at each other, and then one

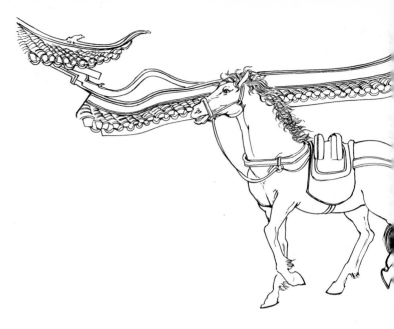

of them came forward and spoke to Liu Bowen. 'I will gladly go,' he said. 'My name is Gaoliang. I was a carpenter by trade before I joined the emperor's army. I am a good rider and will save the emperor's city from harm.'

Giving the soldier a strong lance, Liu Bowen replied, 'You must follow these orders precisely. Ride straight out of the west gate and when you catch up with the old man and his wife, pierce the jars at once and do not say a word. Then turn round and gallop back to Peking as fast as you can. On no account must you look back until you are safely back within the city walls.'

Having received his orders, Gaoliang rode away. He soon picked up the trail of the handcart and eventually he caught up with the old man and his wife. He rode up to them as fast as he could and immediately shattered one of the water jars. But as he pulled his lance back out in order to pierce the second jar, the water gushed out with such force that it threatened to drown him. At the same time there was a loud crash of thunder and the old man resumed his dragon form and looked down at him threateningly. In the noise and confusion Gaoliang realized that, although he had only half completed his task, he had no alternative but to turn round and race back to the city. All the way he could hear the sound of rushing water behind him, as if the water were trying to return

Liu Yi and the dragon king

During the time of the Tang dynasty there lived a student by the name of Liu Yi, who travelled to the capital, Chang'an, to take examinations. Having successfully passed the examinations, he was making his way back to his home near the lakes of central China when he came across a woman beside the road herding sheep. She was a very beautiful young woman, but she looked very sad and had obviously been crying. Liu stopped, got down from his horse and asked her if he could help her in some way. She thanked him for his kindness and, with tears in her eyes, told him her story.

'I am a most unfortunate woman. I am the youngest daughter of the dragon king of Lake Dongting, and my parents married me to the son of the River Jing, who is a worthless man and neglects me entirely. But I cannot complain to my parents-in-law, as they love and admire my husband.' The young woman paused to shed more tears, and then continued her story. 'I know that my father would help me, but I cannot tell him of my unhappiness as Lake Dongting is so far away. I believe that you are heading that way, and I would entrust you to deliver a secret message if you were willing.'

Liu replied, 'I would certainly do anything to serve you, but I am a landbound mortal. How could I ever reach your father in the depths of Lake Dongting? And how would I find him?' 'That will be easy if you are willing to undertake the task. On the northern bank of the lake there is a large tangerine tree, which the local people know to be sacred. When you reach it, tie your belt to the tree and knock on its trunk three times. Then someone will come to lead you to your destination.' With this the young woman handed Liu a letter.

As he put the letter away, Liu said, 'I did not know that immortal dragons herded sheep. Do you also kill animals for food?' 'These are not sheep,' replied the young woman, 'they are rain workers.' 'What does that mean?' asked Liu. 'It means that they make thunder and lightning,' came the reply. Liu looked more closely at the

to the springs and wells of Peking.

Remembering his orders, Gaoliang did not look back, despite all the noise behind him, but galloped straight on to the city. At last he could see the city walls and the figure of Liu Bowen on top of the west wall, calling to him. Thinking that he was now safely home, Gaoliang could not resist taking one look behind him. When he did so, he saw an enormous wave following him and as he looked, the wave rolled right over him and he was drowned.

In later years the people of Peking built a bridge just outside the city to commemorate the young man who had so bravely saved the city. They named the bridge after him, and the Gaoliang bridge stood till recent times.

The jar which Gaoliang failed to pierce contained all the city's sweet spring water, and so it remained in the hills where he caught up with the dragon. This place is still called the Hill of Jade Springs, for there the water is clear and sweet. The water which returned to the city came from the jar containing all the bitter-tasting water from the wells, and though the city does not lack drinking water, even in recent times the water from its wells was bitter. And so, when the people of Peking wanted sweet water to make tea, they always fetched it from beyond the city walls at the Hill of Jade Springs.

animals and, though they held themselves proudly, in other respects their appearance was no different from ordinary sheep.

'I shall gladly be your messenger,' said Liu, 'and when you return to Dongting I hope we shall meet again.' Then he went on his way. When he looked back a bit further down the road, the woman and the sheep were nowhere to be seen.

After he had visited his own home, Liu went immediately to Lake Dongting. He found the tangerine tree just as the young woman had said, and took off his belt and knocked on the tree three times. A short while later he saw a man rise up out of the waves of the lake. The man greeted him politely and asked him where he had come from. Ignoring the question, Liu said firmly, 'I wish to see your king.' Immediately the man parted the waves and led Liu into the lake.

'You must close your eyes for a few minutes,' said the man. Liu did so, and when he opened his eyes again, he found that he was inside the dragon king's palace. There were luxurious halls and high towers with many doors, surrounded by wonderful trees and plants. He saw that everything was covered in pearls and precious stones.

As Liu was admiring the palace, the great doors opened and a regal figure appeared amongst the swirling clouds. This was the dragon king himself and Liu knelt before him. The king greeted him courteously: 'Our dwelling is deep and difficult to reach. What business causes you to brave the journey?' Liu told the king who he was and explained how and where he had met the young woman who had entrusted him with her letter. Then he gave the letter to the king, who opened and read it at once. Weeping and covering his face with his sleeve, the dragon king said, 'I am to blame. I refused to listen to good advice. I sat here and did nothing while my dear young daughter had to suffer so far away. You, sir, are a stranger, but you have helped my daughter when I did not. I shall never forget your kindness.'

The king and all his attendants wept. Then one of them took the letter to the ladies in the rear apartments, and soon the sound of weeping could be heard from there also. The king started and said to one of his attendants, 'Quickly, go and tell them not to make so much noise, or Chiantang will hear them.'

'Who is Chiantang?' asked Liu.

'He is my younger brother,' replied the king. 'He used to be lord of the Chiantang Pool, but now we have to keep him here. He is impetuous beyond belief and his temper has caused many terrible floods. He even quarrelled with the heavenly generals and then tried to flood the Five Holy Peaks of China. Fortunately the High God has forgiven him on my account, so long as I warrant his good behaviour.'

Just as the king finished speaking there was an enormous roar as if the whole world were being torn apart, the palace shook and a huge red dragon rushed through the hall to the accompaniment of thunder, lightning, hail and sleet. In another flash he was gone again, and Liu threw himself on the floor in terror. The dragon king helped him to his feet.

'There is no need to be afraid, he won't harm you,' he said, but in his terror Liu could not answer for some time. Then he said, 'Please take me back to the shore. I would like to be gone before your brother comes back again!'

The king did his best to reassure him. 'His temper will have disappeared by the time he comes back. Please stay for a while and allow us the pleasure of entertaining you.' Then the king called for wine and he and Liu talked about life in the world of mortal men.

A short while later a gentle breeze blew through the hall and the sound of chimes and flutes was heard. A group of women came in, smiling and talking amongst themselves, and Liu saw that the last one of the group was the most beautiful and had the most regal garments. As she approached, he realized that it was the young woman who had given him the letter. 'Ah, here is the prisoner of River Jing,' said the dragon king, embracing the young woman fondly. Then she and the other women went back into the inner palace and a tall, dignified man entered, also in regal clothes. He was introduced to Liu as Chiantang and he treated Liu with the utmost courtesy, thanking him for all he had done to help rescue his niece.

Turning to his brother, Chiantang said, 'Having set out from here in good time, I arrived at the River Jing by noon and we fought there and then. Afterwards I visited the abode of the High

God and explained my actions. He was most understanding and forgave me both for this and my previous wrongdoing. Now I would like you to accept my apologies, brother. I failed to take proper leave of you, caused the most awful commotion in the palace and, worst of all, terrified a most honoured guest. I am filled with shame.'

But the king wanted news of the fight. 'How many people did you kill?' he asked.
'About six hundred thousand,' came the reply.
'How much damage to crops?'
'About eight hundred acres.'
'And what happened to that treacherous son-in-law of mine?' asked the king.
'I ate him,' said his brother. At this the king looked pained. 'That worthless man was certainly quite unbearable, but you were much too hasty. You are very fortunate that the High God saw fit to forgive you. Otherwise, what could I have done? You must not behave in the same way again!' As he left, Chiantang looked suitably chastened.

Next day a feast was held at the palace in Liu's honour, and he was served the most wonderful food and drink, heard the most marvellous music and watched the most graceful girls imaginable. Then the dragon king gave him gifts of pearls and other precious stones, all presented in jade coffers. Chiantang had taken a great liking to Liu and on the following day he also held a feast in his honour. Chiantang drank cup after cup of wine and finally he came towering over Liu and said to him, 'Lord Dongting's daughter is a gentle, tender girl who had the misfortunate to fall amongst ruffians. But now that is all in the past. I would like to give her to you so that we can be linked forever by marriage. She is aware of her debt to you and you are in love with her, so this is the perfect solution.'

Liu felt small and helpless beside this mighty and impetuous dragon who had drunk too much wine. What would he say when he was sober again? Besides, marriage was a serious matter, epecially marriage with an immortal; it was certainly not something to be decided over a cup of wine. Being a cautious young man, Liu spoke seriously and carefully to Chiantang and succeeded in dissuading him from his idea of marriage, whilst they still remained the best of friends.

Next day Liu's hosts reluctantly wished him farewell. When he saw the dragon princess again, Liu was filled with longing despite his coolness the evening before. A score of attendants accompanied Liu to his home, carrying all the gifts with them. Liu grew rich and married, but shortly afterwards his wife died. He married again, but his second wife also died. Then he married a girl from one of the most notable families in the land. As the months passed he came to think that his wife resembled more and more the dragon king's daughter, whom he had not been able to forget. After she had borne him a son, his wife admitted that she was indeed the dragon king's daughter, explaining that she had been very sad when he refused her uncle's offer and could only remember what he had said after their first meeting, 'When you return to Dongting I hope we shall meet again.' Liu was overjoyed.

The couple frequently visited the dragon king's palace in Lake Dongting and people noticed that although he grew old in years, Liu never appeared to age. Finally he and his family went to live in the dragon king's palace forever, and very occasionally he was seen to make an appearance above the waves.

The dragon's pearl

Among the most important of the treasures belonging to a guardian dragon was a magic pearl. This was so precious that he kept it always near him in his pool, sometimes in his mouth or under his chin. The pearl was full of magic powers: it gave off a radiant light that never faded and made things among which it was placed increase and multiply. The following story tells what happened when one dragon's pearl fell into human hands.

Many centuries ago by the side of the River Min in the province of Sichuan there lived a mother and her son. They were poor people and the mother was old, sickly and almost blind. She spent most of her time at home, whilst her fourteen year old son wandered through the hills and countryside cutting grass, which he then sold as animal fodder or fuel. In this way they just managed to live.

One summer there was a terrible drought and life became even harder for them. The boy wandered the hills as usual, but could find barely enough grass to buy a little food for his mother and himself. Then high up in the hills, beside a stream that was almost dried up, he came across a large patch of the most luscious green grass that he had ever seen. The grass was tall and sturdy, better even than in good years, and he quickly cut the whole patch, hoisted the grass onto his back and carried it to the village. There he was able to sell the grass for more money than he usually received for a whole day's work.

Next day his wanderings took him again to the same spot in the hills, where to his amazement he saw that the grass had sprung up again, as thick and luscious as the day before. He quickly cut the whole patch again and took the grass to the village. On the third day the same thing happened again, and the boy felt very happy with his marvellous patch of grass.

The only thing which he did not like, however, was the distance from his house to the patch of grass, which gave him such a long, rough journey every day. Then it occurred to him that, if this was a magic patch of grass, it should grow just as well beside his house. He decided to find out, and

so the very next day he made several journeys into the hills, transporting the earth and roots to his house. As he was digging out the roots he found amongst the grass a large brilliant pearl tinged with pink. He took this treasure home to show to his mother and together they admired its beauty and brilliance, deciding to keep it for a little while before selling it in the nearest city. They were sure that it would fetch the largest sum of money that they had ever seen.

The old woman put the pearl in the jar where they kept their rice. As usual there was not very much rice in the jar, just enough for one more meal. Then her son carried on planting the earth and roots beside the house, forgetting all about the pearl. He was very tired from his hard day's work and, when he had finished, went straight to bed. Next morning he leaped out of bed and rushed outside to see how the grass had grown, only to find that it had not grown at all, but was withered and dying. The boy wept in despair, blaming himself for having moved the grass from the hills and wondering where he would now find any grass at all.

Suddenly he remembered the pearl, and began to wonder whether that might have something to do with it. Going back into the house, he went straight to the rice jar where his mother had put the pearl. To his astonishment he found that the jar was full to the brim with rice. The pearl was still there, gleaming on top of the rice as if it were smiling. He called his mother, and the two of them rejoiced together. They decided to try the

pearl out again, and so they emptied the rice jar, leaving just a handful at the bottom, replaced the pearl and put on the lid. Next morning they were delighted to find the jar brimming over with rice once again. Realizing that this was a magic pearl, they agreed to keep the knowledge to themselves and to put the pearl to good use. That night they put the pearl in the box where they kept their money and, sure enough, next morning the box was overflowing with coins. Then they tried the bottle where they kept their oil, and next day it was full of the best quality oil. Using the pearl carefully, the mother and son became quite wealthy, and the boy did not have to go out cutting grass again.

Naturally their good fortune was noticed by their neighbours, for they no longer had to beg and borrow. Indeed, they were now very generous in giving and lending to those who had been kind to them. At first the neighbours wondered where their wealth had come from, but eventually their secret was discovered. Unfortunately not all their neighbours took an honest interest in the affair, and some men came to the house, begging and bullying the poor old woman and her son to show them the pearl. As they were simple people, they did not know how to resist these bullies and in the end the boy took the pearl from its hiding place and showed it to them on the palm of his hand. As the men crowded round to get a look at the pearl, the boy could see that they meant no good and, without thinking, he quickly put the pearl into his mouth.

One of the men then grabbed him by the shoulders and shook him hard, shouting at him to spit the pearl out. Unfortunately, this had the opposite effect and the boy swallowed the pearl.

As the pearl travelled down to the boy's stomach, he felt a terrible burning sensation inside, as though he were swallowing a ball of fire. He was consumed with the most terrible thirst and, grabbing the teapot, he emptied it in one draught. Then he rushed to the large water jar and, pouring twenty to thirty ladlefuls of water down his throat, he emptied the jar. Still he was thirsty and he next ran to the well and hauled up as many buckets as he could, till the well was completely dry. Still he was thirsty, in fact even more thirsty than before. He ran down to the river like a man possessed, threw himself down on the bank and drank the water as fast as he could.

His mother could only watch him in distress, and she pleaded with him to stop drinking. But she and the neighbours watched in horror as he drank the river completely dry. As he did so, there was a loud crash of thunder, a wind sprang up and the sky was full of lightning and rain. The earth began to tremble, and the people fell to the ground in fear. The young boy was shaking, and his mother took hold of his legs as they started to grow in size. Scales began to sprout on his back, horns appeared on his head and with staring eyes he grew bigger and bigger. The woman saw that her son was turning into a dragon before her very eyes, and she knew that it was the pearl that had done this to him.

The unfortunate woman hung onto her son's leg desperately, and the dragon tried not to shake her off too violently as the rain continued to pour down. The river was filling up again and the dragon managed to throw his mother off onto the bank. As he went into the river, he could hear her desperate cries behind him and he could not stop himself from looking round. Each time she wailed he turned round, and the mighty thrust and coil of his huge body as he turned round to look at her created large mud banks on the river bed.

These mud banks are still there, bearing witness to the dragon's last farewell to his mother as he disappeared into the river for ever. In memory of this event the people of the area still call these mud banks the 'Looking at Mother Banks'.

Buddhist tales

The Buddhist religion came to China from India in about the first century AD but did not become established there until some centuries later. Buddhism introduced many new things to China, new ways of thinking and new gods including Buddha himself and the popular Goddess of Mercy, Guanyin. The Chinese people adapted the new religion to their own way of life, linking it with their own ancient beliefs to produce myths and stories that were a mixture of native and foreign elements.

Buddhism brought a great change in Chinese thought. One of its most important ideas was the concept of a cyclical life in which humans are reincarnated in different forms according to the way they have behaved, so that a person who has sinned might find himself born again in the form of an animal or an insect. Buddhism also brought a new sense of respect for all living things, leading to vegetarianism as people began to refuse to kill animals for food. So deeply were people affected by the new religion that many became monks and nuns, dedicating their lives to prayer, worship and good deeds.

Guanyin, or Kwanyin, the Chinese Goddess of Mercy, was originally an Indian Buddhist deity by the name of Avalokitesvara. When Buddhist missionaries travelled eastwards from India via Tibet to China, the deity's name was translated as Guanyin, meaning 'the one who now looks down upon the world and hears its cries' and symbolizing mercy. Until about the twelfth century Guanyin was usually thought of as a male god, as he had been in India, but gradually, perhaps because the quality of mercy was associated in China more with the feminine than the masculine character, the deity came to be represented as a goddess.

Guanyin was worshipped as a saviour, especially from the perils of the sea and as a giver of children. It is possible that the earlier Chinese gods and goddesses responsible for these aspects of human life had been absorbed into her powerful figure. No other god held as important a place in popular worship as Guanyin. Her image was to be found in many homes, and there were shrines and temples to her everywhere, eclipsing even the supreme god Buddha himself. The cult of Guanyin is centred at Putuo on the island of Zhoushan off the coast of Zhejiang in central China, and though evidence points to her being an imported goddess, many people believe that she was originally an ancient Chinese princess called Miaoshan. The story begins with her father.

In ancient times there lived a king called Miaozhuang, who ruled over many regions in the west of China. He and his wife had two daughters and the king was anxious to have a son to succeed him on the throne. He offered prayers and sacrifices to the gods in the hope of having an heir, but though a third child was born, the king was disappointed to learn that it was another daughter. They named the little girl Miaoshan.

From birth Miaoshan showed herself to be a good Buddhist by refusing to eat meat. As she grew up, the little princess was loved by everyone, for she was modest, kind and always cheerful. Her one ambition in life was to become a Buddhist nun and to devote her life to religion, but as a princess she was not allowed to do this. Both her older sisters were married to princes, and before very long the king found a suitable match for Miaoshan. When his daughter refused to get married, the king became so angry that he ordered his wife to strip Miaoshan of her warm clothing and lock her out in the courtyard behind the palace without any food. This the queen did, but Miaoshan did not give in. In fact the prison was to her liking; she was left in peace to say her prayers, her body soon grew used to the cold, and she could drink dew and eat plants.

When they saw that the punishment was having no effect on Miaoshan, the king and queen begged her to remember that it was her duty to obey them. But she was determined not to marry and asked to be allowed instead to enter a nearby convent, where five hundred nuns lived a life of devotion. Seeing no alternative, the king finally gave his permission, but he secretly ordered the abbess to give his daughter the most menial and unpleasant tasks in the convent so that she would no longer want to be a nun. The orders were carried out, but again they had no effect on Miaoshan. Her determination was so strong that the gods in Heaven, particularly a powerful god known as the Jade Emperor, sent spirits down to earth to help her with her tasks, so that it required little effort on her part to complete all that she was asked to do. When the abbess reported this to the

king, he grew so angry that he ordered his soldiers to go and burn down the convent, with his daughter inside it. As flames rose around the frightened nuns, Miaoshan prayed to Buddha and he sent down a heavy shower of rain to put out the fire and save them all.

At this the king was thrown into a terrible rage, and he ordered that Miaoshan be killed. The princess was happy that she would now be going to Heaven and as the soldiers carried out the execution, the Jade Emperor sent down a god in the form of a tiger to take her body to a dark forest. Her soul went down to the Underworld like other human souls but her saintliness turned even that dismal place into a paradise, so that all the condemned souls were reprieved. The gods of the Underworld were so upset by this that they urgently asked Buddha to take her away again, and he had her carried away to Putuo where her soul was reunited with her body. There she rested and meditated, and through her prayers she became sublime and perfect. She was able to float out of her own body and to see things which others could not see. In this way she was able to rescue many people from danger.

Once she was able to rescue the son of the dragon king of the Southern Sea, who had taken the form of a carp. He had been caught by fishermen and was being offered for sale at the market but Miaoshan sent her attendants to buy the fish and have it released back into the sea. The dragon king was so grateful for this that he gave Miaoshan a beautiful pearl by which she could see in the dark.

Meanwhile her father had been stricken by a plague of boils all over his body as a result of his wickedness towards his own daughter. He was suffering terrible pain and the doctors could find no medicine with which to cure him. When Miaoshan learned of this, she went to her father disguised as a Buddhist monk. She told him that the only cure would be to have an eye and a hand from a living person.
'This person must be perfect in holiness,' she said, 'and you will find such a one at Putuo on the island of Zhoushan.'

The king was grateful for the advice and immediately sent to Putuo. While he was waiting for his attendants to return, his two sons-in-law

plotted to kill him for they did not want him to recover from his illness. Miaoshan saw this and informed the king, who had his sons-in-law put to death at once.

Miaoshan spoke to the king's attendants when they arrived at Putuo. 'Cut an eye and a hand from my own person and take them to the king.' This they did, but it was found that this cured only one side of the king's body, and the attendants were sent to fetch the other eye and hand. Once more these were given by Miaoshan, and on the attendants' return the king was completely cured. When the king asked them to describe the holy person who had made this supreme sacrifice, they said that she was very like his own daughter Miaoshan. The king knew at once that it must have been her, and he vowed to make a pilgrimage to Putuo with his family.

Three years later they did indeed make the pilgrimage, and when the king saw his daughter's mutilated body, he fell down before her. As his wife and daughters wept, the king begged to know how her body could be restored. 'If you would but worship Heaven, father,' said Miaoshan, 'admit your guilt, offer repentance and promise to lead a pure and holy life, then I shall be made whole again.'

To this the king replied, 'I have committed a monstrous crime against my own daughter, and yet she has sacrificed herself in order to restore me to health. I vow that from this day I shall lead a pure and holy life.'

At these words Miaoshan's body was made whole and she embraced her father and mother. From then on the king, the queen and the three princesses led pure, blameless lives, and by the order of the Jade Emperor, Miaoshan was from that day known as Guanyin, the merciful, compassionate protectress of mortals and queen of the seas.

Mulien rescues his mother

The Chinese Buddhist concept of the Underworld is closely bound up with the idea that the soul passes through many stages. The Underworld represented a phase during which the soul would be punished for its sins, purified and prepared for the next phase in its journey towards the Western Paradise. The ruler of the Underworld was a god, Yama, whose Chinese name was Yenlo Wang, and the Underworld itself—Hell—lay deep beneath the surface of the earth, some said under the province of Sichuan.

People based their idea of the Underworld on the Chinese system of justice and punishment, and it was divided up in the same way. There were ten panels or courts of judges and a large number of individual hells, up to as many as a hundred, with appropriate punishments for the sinners who were sentenced to occupy them. The guards who fetched men from the world of the living, who attended on the judges and who administered the punishments were very frightening creatures indeed. There were spectres with human arms and legs but the heads of horses and oxen, and there were devils with various kinds of monstrous heads and red hair, a colour unknown amongst the Chinese people.

Everyone had to pass through the Underworld, but there were ways of making the passage through it less painful. Relatives of the dead would try to make amends for the sins of members of their family by saying prayers on their behalf and doing good deeds, such as making donations to temples. In this way the dead soul's suffering could be eased. The following story shows how one man saved his mother by prayer and holiness.

There was once a rich man who, being a fervent disciple of Buddha, lived in a pure and holy way, was kind to both men and animals and refused ever to eat meat. His wife and son lived in the same way, and the family was happy and prosperous. The man lived to a ripe old age and, when he died, he was transported by cranes to the Western Paradise, where he would spend the rest of time living in bliss in the Buddhist fashion. After his father's death, the son, Lobu, was called

away to a foreign land on business, but before he left he gave part of his inheritance to his mother, telling her to use it to feed any needy monks who might come to her door.

Without the encouragement of her husband and son, the mother, whose name was Chingti, began to stray from the strict discipline of a Buddhist life. She began to enjoy eating meat, and killed all kinds of animals for food, including even a dog. And she showed no hospitality to the monks who came to her door, giving one starving monk leftovers from her table contaning meat, so that the unfortunate man committed a heinous sin without knowing it. She simply drove other monks away from her door, keeping her son's money for her own use. When Lobu returned from abroad he asked his mother if she had used the money as he had ordered, and she assured him that she had, thus adding another sin to those which she had already committed. She died not long afterwards and was sent down to the Underworld. There she was put in one of the worst punishment hells called the Avici.

After mourning his mother's death and giving her a proper burial, Lobu left his home to become a monk, a thing he had not done before as he felt that he owed a duty to his parents. Now that they were both dead, he thought that it was time to follow his calling. When he was accepted as a monk, his head was shaved, he put on a cassock and he was given the new name of Mulien. He soon became so wise and pious that he was one of the best loved of Buddha's disciples. One of his achievements was the ability to move through all levels of existence, on earth, in Heaven, in the Buddhist paradises, and through the multiple layers of the Underworld. When he first had command of this skill, he travelled to the Western Paradise and conversed with his father, who was very pleased to see him, but he was unable to find his mother anywhere in Heaven. He was sad at this and went to ask Buddha where his mother was.

'Mulien,' said Buddha, 'your mother has fallen into the Avici hell and is suffering for her sins on earth. Although you have reached a high level of piety and can perform miracles, there is nothing you can do to save her, unless all the monks in the

world should one day sing prayers for her in concert and thereby gain her release.'

This news came as a sad shock to Mulien, who nevertheless decided that he must rescue his mother from the Underworld. He used his special powers to descend into the Underworld, and the first people he saw were a group of men and women wandering about dolefully with nothing to do. Mulien asked them what they were doing and if they had seen Chingti, his mother. The people said that they had not seen her, and then one of them gave a sad account of their own predicament. 'We are the unfortunate victims of a terrible mistake. We were on earth and not due to die, but because our names are the same as some of those in the Book of the Dead, we were seized and brought down here, though we cannot even be admitted into the Underworld. Our earthly bodies have already been buried, so we cannot return there either. That is why we are wandering here like lost souls. Our relatives mourn for us and make expensive sacrifices, but these do us no good. The only thing that might help is if they were to do good deeds in our names.' The lost souls continued to lament, and directed Mulien to the court of King Yama.

He went through the triple gates into the kingdom of Yama, thronged with large groups of people. He searched everywhere but, unable to find his mother, he shed bitter tears. Seeing this, the attendants at the gates led him to King Yama himself, who rose and greeted him with great respect.
'Your holiness, what brings a pious man such as yourself to this place of suffering? What is it that you wish?'
'I seek my mother,' replied Mulien. 'I have sought her in vain in Heaven, and now I must seek her here. Have you seen her?' The king did not know where she was, but he called all his subordinates before him and asked them if they knew. They were able to tell Mulien that his mother had committed great sins on earth and that her records had been sent to the General of the Five Ways.

And so Mulien set off again. He had not gone far when he reached the River of No Hope, where souls were waiting to cross and were being driven about by demons with animal heads and fierce faces. Some people had taken off their clothes so

as to swim across the river, but they were not allowed to do so, whilst others were being herded together. The weeping and lamenting filled Mulien with pity and terror, and he hurried on with tears in his eyes. Finally he arrived at the office of the General of the Five Ways, the fiercest and most cruel of all the judges in the Underworld. In reply to Mulien's questions, the General sent for his subordinates, and one officer said, 'There was a woman of that description about three years ago, and she was claimed by the Avici authorities. I expect that is where she is now.'

Mulien asked, 'How is it that King Yama does not know my mother's fate, since everyone must report to him before doing anything else?'
'That is not so,' replied the General. 'All those who die are first divided into good people and evil people. The good ascend straight up to Heaven without further ado, and the evil go straight to their appropriate punishment in Hell. Only those people who are neither totally good nor evil come before King Yama, and he must decide what form of punishment they deserve and in what form

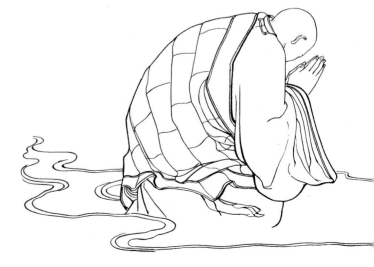

they will be reborn, according to how good or evil they have been.'

Mulien then left the General and made his way towards the terrible Avici hell. On his way he passed many different hells, each one for a different sin, some containing men, some women and some both. At each one he stopped to ask after his mother, and as he drew nearer to the Avici hell he could see scores of demons swarming about.

'Do not enter here, monk,' they warned. 'A foul mist rises from the heart of this hell and will turn your flesh to ashes.' At this, Mulien rose up from the Underworld and made his way back to Buddha, asking if he could borrow his staff to protect himself from harm. Then he returned once more to the Avici hell, where there were flames licking everywhere and arrows flying about in strong winds to tear at people's flesh.

Taking Buddha's staff, Mulien beat upon the doors and they opened at once. The custodian of the doors asked him what he wanted, and when Mulien asked again after his mother, the custodian climbed to the top of a tower, hoisted a

white flag and beat on an iron drum. 'Is there a woman here called Chingti?' he shouted. As there was no reply, he went to the next compound, climbed another tower, hoisted a black flag, beat on the iron drum and asked again. He carried on in this way till he came to the seventh compound, where he hoisted a green flag and asked, 'Is there a woman called Chingti in this compound?' This time she was there, suffering torture on a bed of nails, but she did not dare reply. But when the custodian beat again on his drum and asked for the second time, she replied, 'I am she.'

'Why did you not answer before?' asked the custodian.

'I was afraid to,' replied Chingti. 'I thought you might take me somewhere else for even worse torments.'

'Outside the door,' said the custodian, 'there is a young monk with a shaven head who says he is your son.' For a long time Chingti was silent and then she finally said, 'I have no son who is a monk, it must be a mistake.'

The custodian went back to Mulien and said, 'Monk, why are you claiming this woman as your mother, and why are you lying to me?'

'Let me explain,' said Mulien. 'My former name was Lobu and it was only after my parents died that I became a monk and was given the name of Mulien.' When Chingti was told this, she knew that it must indeed be her son and she was taken to the gate. Mulien was horrified when he saw her. Blood was pouring from wounds all over her body, flames were licking around her and even coming out of her mouth, and she looked half starved. The first thing that he could think of was to ask, 'Did you not receive the offerings of food that I sacrificed for you?' To this his mother replied, 'How could they reach me in this torture? You may have gained satisfaction and a reputation for piety by making the offerings, but they did me no good. It might have helped if you had copied out some sutras in my name.'

The custodian came to take her away and although Mulien offered to suffer in her place in the Avici hell, this was not allowed and he had to leave her to her torments. Mulien then went to Buddha to plead for his mother, and out of respect for the monk, Buddha went down to the Underworld, where his radiance dispelled the gloom and horror and the torment melted away. The souls of the damned were released and transferred to Heaven, but unfortunately this came too late for Mulien's mother. She was already doomed to walk the earth as a hungry ghost, with all food and drink turning instantly to ashes as soon as it touched her lips. She begged Mulien for food, as the rules relating to hungry ghosts did not apply to food given as alms to a monk. Her son rushed off with his begging bowl and returned with alms, but this also turned to ashes when his mother tried to eat it. He therefore felt obliged to go and seek the help of Buddha once again.

Buddha repeated what he had said to Mulien previously. 'All the monks must sing prayers for her together,' he said. Mulien set about organizing the festival of Yülanpen. On the fifteenth day of the seventh month, all the priests and monks joined in prayer at all the temples, praying for the souls of the dead. This unison of prayer was particularly helpful for the souls in hell, and on that day all hungry ghosts were at last able to eat one meal. Since that time the festival has been held wherever there are Buddhist believers.

After she had eaten at last, Chingti again disappeared. This time Buddha came to Mulien and told him, 'Through your piety and holiness in organizing the Yülanpen festival, your mother has been released from being a hungry ghost. She has already been reincarnated, but according to her deserts could rise no higher than the form of a dog. If you wish to see her again, go to the city of Wangshe and walk before the doors of the rich pious men. A black dog will come out, tugging at your cassock and speaking with a human tongue. That dog will be your mother, Chingti.'

Mulien went to Wangshe and everything happened exactly as Buddha had said it would. The black dog rushed out of the house and took hold of his cassock.

'My son,' she said. 'You have saved me from the torments of hell. Will you not also save me from this dog's life?'

'Dear mother,' replied Mulien. 'It was my lack of piety which caused you to fall into such torments. But compared with your earlier suffering, are you not happier as a dog?'

'It is true,' replied Chingti. 'To hear my masters reciting the scriptures and saying prayers each morning, and never to hear the word "hell" even mentioned, this more than makes up for the impurities of life as a dog.'

Then Mulien led her to the pagoda before the temple in the town, and for seven days and nights he recited the scriptures without ceasing. As a result of this, Chingti was able to leave the form of a dog, hanging the dog's skin on a tree, and resuming the form of a healthy woman. Mulien was overjoyed, and begged his mother, 'Now that you once more have the form of a human being, I beg you, mother, to act piously and to make yourself deserving of this reincarnation.'

After a time Mulien took his mother before Buddha and, walking round him three times in the forest of holy sala trees, asked, 'Honoured one, please examine my mother's destiny to see if there remain any sins for which she has not made amends.' Buddha did as he was requested and acknowledged that Chingti had paid the penalty of all her sins and that they had been expiated by the monks at the festival of Yülanpen. And so at last, amidst great rejoicing, she was welcomed into the Western Paradise.

The monk Huiyuan

Many stories are told about the deeds of Buddhists of the past who were famous for their piety and their knowledge and teaching of the Buddhist scriptures, the sutras. One of these was the monk Huiyuan, who lived from 334 to 416AD and founded the White Lotus sect which taught that there was a paradise in the west for believers.

After many years of studying the sutras, Huiyuan left his master to preach and spread the message of the sutras throughout the land. As he journeyed he came to the mountain of Lushan, one of the great peaks of China, in the province of Hubei in central China. He was delighted with the mountain scenery and while he was there felt his powers of concentration increase and his whole being draw nearer to Buddha. He made his home on Lushan and built a small shelter where he spent his days meditating and reciting the

sutras. The resonant tones of his voice carried a long way and the spirits of the mountain and the trees listened to his words. They were so impressed by what they heard that in a day and a night of thunder and flashing lightning, they built him a marvellous temple.

Huiyuan was astounded to see such a fine temple appear from nothing but, rightly attributing it to the powers of the sutras, he thanked Buddha and walked inside to inspect it. Everything seemed perfect except that there was no water supply. As he walked down from the main hall of worship he noticed a flat rock and struck it with his monk's staff which was made of tin. Immediately a spring gushed out and to this day the spring provides water for the monastery and is still called the Spring of the Tin Staff. Its clear water flows away to a pool called the White Lotus Pool.

Huiyuan took up residence in the temple and soon gathered many disciples. People came from far and wide to listen to him preaching; even the spirits came in human form to hear him, vanishing into thin air as soon as the sermon was over. Huiyuan's fame spread.

Then disaster struck. The monastery was overrun by bands of brigands led by a man called Bo Zhuang who had heard how popular the temple was and decided to take its riches for himself. The monks all ran away but Huiyuan was taken prisoner and made a slave. He had to serve the brigand chief for several years, with no time to read the sutras or to meditate. One day the brigands were encamped on a hillside and Huiyuan was asleep. In a dream he saw Buddha appear to him in all his glory, exhorting him to return to his duty of explaining the sutras and converting unbelievers to Buddhism. Buddha told him that he would soon be sold to a new master and that all his troubles were to expiate a debt he owed to a man in a former existence. This man was destined to be his new master.

Everything happened as Buddha had said. Huiyuan's life changed once more, for the new master was a government minister. Once again Huiyuan was able to attend Buddhist services and listen to the sermons.

One day Huiyuan's master took him to hear a very popular preacher named Dao An. Huiyuan found Dao An's interpretation of the sutras mistaken and shallow and his master, noticing that he was weeping, asked him the reason for his distress. Huiyuan explained who he was and showed a birthmark on his arm which proved that he was indeed the great master who had been abducted by brigands many years before. The minister was a good man and he arranged at once for Huiyuan to be publicly restored to his position at Lushan, where he ruled over a great community of monks and followers until he died.

The world in a pillow

One of the ideas that came to China with Buddhism was a consciousness that life on earth is just a short phase in the life of the soul, a fleeting moment compared to the slow changes of the universe. With this consciousness came a new assessment of the value of wealth and power: however rich or famous a person becomes everything vanishes when he dies, so that the poorest beggar dies with no less than the richest king. The story that follows shows this most clearly.

During the time of the Tang dynasty there was a country inn at Handan, which was situated in the north-western part of China. One day a young man by the name of Lu arrived at this country inn. He was riding a black mare, having just come from the fields, and wore a short, rough coat. At the inn Lu shared a table with an old man who had travelled a very long way, and after a while they fell into conversation. After much talking and laughing together, the young man began to feel that he had known the old man all his life.

Then Lu looked down at his own shabby clothes, sighed and said, 'What sort of a miserable life is this for a man?'

The old man looked at him in surprise and said, 'I can see nothing wrong with you in either body or spirit. What is it that troubles you?' The young man sighed again and replied, 'With such a poor life as mine, how can a man be happy?' 'If what you have is not enough,' said the old man, 'tell me what it is that would make you happy.' Lu replied at once, 'In this world a real man should make a name for himself, gain riches and enjoy honour, making his family wealthy and powerful. I am already a grown man and, although I am skilful with weapons, all I have done is till the fields and I can achieve nothing more.'

As he spoke, his eyes began to feel heavy and he rubbed them as if he were feeling tired. He looked round the inn and saw that the landlord was cooking millet porridge for some of the guests. The old man at the table made room for him on the couch on which he was sitting, and said, 'Come, I can see you are tired. Why not have a sleep? Use my pillow; it will make you rich and famous, as you desire.' The pillow was made of green pottery, as was usual in those days in China, and there was a small hole at both ends. Lu put his head on the pillow to sleep.

As he lay there, it seemed to him that the hole at one end of the pillow was growing bigger and bigger, letting light in from the other end. It became so big that Lu was able to walk right into the pillow and back out through the holes. When he did so, he found himself walking away from the inn on the road home.

A few months later Lu married a beautiful girl from a rich family in the neighbourhood, and his family increased in wealth. Then he acquired a good job and was quickly promoted until he became a provincial governor. In a few years he was promoted several more times, held offices in various provinces, and finally was given a senior post in the capital. At that time the Tibetans were attacking the Chinese border and the general of the Chinese army had been defeated

and killed. Lu was given command of the army and he soon drove back the invaders and made the border safe. The grateful border people built a commemorative tablet to him and he received many honours from the emperor himself.

Within ten years Lu had risen to a very powerful position and was one of the most influential men in the land. Such a person is never without malicious critics, and Lu was falsely accused of having acted as a spy for foreigners. The emperor immediately ordered his imprisonment and, when the guards came to take him away, he turned to his wife in tears and said, 'Once my family owned but a few acres of land in the provinces and had to work hard to clothe and feed us . Why was I so ambitious and greedy for more? Now I would give anything to be a simple man again, riding on my black mare in my short, rough coat.' He wept and took a knife to put an end to his own life, but his wife stopped him. Later the emperor released him from prison, but ordered him to be banished.

In time the people who had accused Lu died and finally the emperor learned the truth. He recalled Lu to the capital and heaped honours on him once again. Lu became the head of a large and powerful family, with five sons who had married into noble families, and who held high offices. More than fifty years passed by with Lu living a life of luxury. Finally his health deteriorated and even the emperor's own doctors could not help him. On his death bed he sent a message commending himself to his majesty the emperor, and received an honourable reply. A few hours later he died.

At that moment Lu woke with a yawn. He saw that he was still lying on the couch at the wayside inn, next to the old man who had lent him his pillow. The guests were still waiting for the landlord's porridge, which was not yet cooked, and everything else looked just the same. Lu looked round in amazement. 'Is it possible that I dreamed all that?' he asked the old man.
'The passing of a man's life is just like that,' said the old man. Lu was silent for a long time, and at last he thanked the old man for allowing him to experience power and riches, poverty and degradation, life and death, and for fulfilling his desires. Then he bowed to the old man and left.

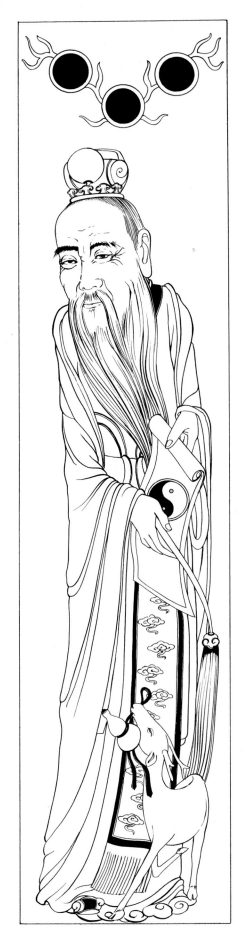

Taoist tales of magic and fantasy

Taoism was the earliest religion of China and some of the Taoist gods and goddesses go right back to the very beginnings of ancient Chinese mythology. Amongst them was the Queen Mother of the West, the fearsome goddess with the face of a woman, the teeth of a tiger and the tail of a leopard who guarded the sacred peach tree on Mount Kunlun and gave the elixir of immortality to Yi the Archer. Although eventually thought of as gods and goddesses, these early spirits were at first much simpler beings. In very ancient times the Chinese mused upon the power of nature and the way in which the elements—even inanimate objects—seemed to assume a power of their own. It is much the same attitude that today makes us call a ship 'she' and makes us angry with a vacuum cleaner or a washing machine for not functioning properly, just as if they were real people. In an attempt to explain this, the Chinese came to believe that everything, including inanimate objects, had a guardian spirit who might be either well or badly disposed towards human beings. The system of worship that grew up was designed to propitiate these guardian spirits, to prevent them from acting in a way that would harm the people with whom they came into contact. Eventually the guardian spirits became gods and goddesses and stories grew up around many of them.

Taoist religion explained the world by means of supernatural beings but there was also a school of Taoist philosophy which tried to make sense of the laws of nature without bringing in spirits or gods at all. Taoist philosophers believed in a natural order that governed the movements and behaviour of everything in the world, whether it was a human being, a bird, a piece of wood or stone or a gust of wind. The Taoist philosopher's aim was to study the natural laws that governed the universe and to try to order his own life accordingly. One of the clearest expressions of their great feeling for nature is in Chinese landscape painting, where Taoist masters are shown communing with nature, far from the influence of people who were often seen as disrupters of the harmony and order of the natural world.

One of the earliest Taoist written documents was a book that came to be known as the *Tao Te Ching*. Originally this was probably a collection of sayings but over hundreds of years the text was changed as scribes copied it out again and again. Some parts have been lost all together, others are incomplete and the book is often quite impossible to understand. To followers of the Taoist religion, this did not matter—in fact it added to the book's mystery and it came to be used as a series of magic charms. The man who was thought to have written the book, Laozi, was worshipped as a god and considered to have all kinds of magic powers.

The Taoist religion took new gods from local Chinese cults and even from other religions such as Buddhism which came originally from outside China. Over the years the new ideas and new gods were completely absorbed and were soon just as 'Chinese' as the ancient Taoist figures. As new details were added the gods became more and more colourful and fantastic and tales about them are full of their extraordinary powers—their ability to fly, to disappear into thin air, to fight using the elements of nature, or command armies made out of paper. In the end the gods came to be treated rather like superior magicians or conjurors, yet many of the fascinating tales that are told about them have more serious meanings and deal with important human relationships. The story of Prince Nocha is one of these. The plot is full of spirits and magic but at a deeper level it is concerned with a basic Chinese attitude towards the relationship between a father and his son. Although the story claims to date from prehistoric times, it was actually written about the sixteenth century when Taoist beliefs had become full of magic and fantasy.

Prince Nocha

During the ancient Shang period there lived a general named Li Ching. Li's wife was expecting a baby but had carried the child for three and a half years without giving birth. One night she dreamed that a Taoist priest stole into her room and thrust something into her bosom. The dream was so vivid that it woke her and she had only just time to rouse her husband and explain the dream to him before she at last went into labour.

Li left the room very worried both by the dream and by his wife's unusual pregnancy. Soon he heard shouts from inside: his wife had given birth to a monster. Rushing back into the bedroom, he saw a strange mass of flesh whirling round, giving out a glowing red light. Without a second thought he struck at it with his sword, releasing from it a small, fair-skinned child with a red silken band tied around its waist.

The child was put to bed and next day the Taoist god Taiyi, the spirit of the Northern Pole Star, came and adopted the child as his disciple, for he was in fact the incarnation of a heavenly pearl. The child remained in the care of his earthly parents who called him Nocha and, in spite of his strange birth, tried to treat him as a normal son.

Nocha, however, was no ordinary child. By the time he was seven he was already six feet tall and very strong. One summer's day he was out walking by a clear pool. The sun was very hot and he took off his clothes and dipped the silk band he still wore around his waist into the water so that he could cool himself with it. The silk band's magical qualities had a terrible effect. A shock like that of a great earthquake shook the pool, shattering the palace of a dragon king who lived deep in the water.

Of course the dragon king sent one of his guards up to find out what was happening and Nocha instantly killed him. When the guard failed to return, the dragon king sent up his own son and Nocha struck him down, too, with one powerful blow. Finally the dragon king assumed the form of a man and went to find Li Ching to complain about what had taken place.
'Nocha, is this true?' asked Li sternly. 'Did you kill the dragon king's son?'
'Oh yes,' replied Nocha carelessly. 'In fact I believe there were two of them. But the first one looked more like a servant to me. Why? Is something the matter?'

Li and his wife were speechless as, in a terrible voice, the dragon king vowed to avenge the deaths of his people.

Puzzled, Nocha went to find his master Taiyi to ask his advice.
'The wrong is done now,' said Taiyi, 'and must be avenged. Return at once to your parents, for the dragon king plans to kill them in payment for the lives you so carelessly wasted.'

Nocha ran back back to his home and, in order

to save his parents, offered to pay with his own life. The dragon king accepted and Nocha killed himself.

Nocha's spirit went once more to his master Taiyi. 'How can I return, master?' he asked. 'Your mother must build a temple for you,' replied Taiyi, 'and you must dwell there for three years. After that you may be reincarnated.'

Nocha appeared to his mother in a dream and told her what Taiyi had said, but when she told Li, he forbade her to have anything to do with such a plan. All he wanted to do was to forget the monstrous son who had brought them so much trouble. However, Nocha did not give up. He came to his mother again and again until she could scarcely close her eyes without seeing his familiar face and hearing his quiet, pleading voice. At last she built a temple secretly and dedicated it to him.

The temple was popular and had many worshippers; Nocha's spirit remained there preparing for reincarnation. Then one day Li happened to pass by.
'To whom does this fine temple belong?' he asked one of the worshippers.

'It is Nocha's,' came the reply, 'Nocha the heavenly pearl who killed himself to save his parents from the dragon king. He lives here, cleansing his spirit so that he can return to earth.' 'May that day never dawn,' cried Li and he immediately set about smashing all the images in the temple. In his anger he burned the temple to the ground.

Nocha was furious at what his father had done to the temple, especially as he considered that by killing himself, he had fully paid for his crime. He decided to punish Li in his turn.

Nocha's spirit had by now assumed a different form. He was sixteen feet fall and had eight arms, each wielding a different kind of weapon. Under his feet were wheels of fire and a great wind carried him swiftly through the air wherever he wanted to go. In this terrible shape he descended on his father, determined to kill him. The Taoist gods could not tolerate this behaviour, even in one of their disciples and they sent a god down to save Li. At first the god tried to reason with Nocha, but Nocha was too angry to listen. Li had no hope of defeating this whirling monster by

himself so the god gave him a miniature pagoda containing a magic talisman which sent Nocha spinning and tumbling away whenever he tried to come near. Nocha returned reluctantly to his master to learn how to control his fiery temper and to use his power in a less destructive way.

Li was saved and later he, too, became immortal, as a Taoist fighting god. He was reconciled with Nocha and together they helped the new king of the Chou dynasty to found the Chinese state and empire. Although they were once more friends, Li was never quite sure he could trust his son and he always carried with him the pagoda with its magic talisman. Because of this he came to be known as Li the Pagoda Bearer.

Zhang Daoling

Many of the features of Taoist religious beliefs were associated with magic, and a Taoist was not considered proficient until he had so mastered the laws of nature that he could rise above them, performing magic feats such as flying through the air, conjuring up objects or becoming invisible. These mysteries were passed on from a master to his disciples, and one story tells of how a man left his home and family to follow such a Taoist master.

After serving his master for several years, the man tired of his menial duties, which seemed to him to have nothing to do with Taoism, and decided to return home. His master had not been very happy with him as a Taoist and was glad to be rid of him, but the disciple begged to be taught something before he left which would give him at least one skill to show for his years of apprenticeship.

'Could you not at least teach me how to walk through a wall without using the door?' he asked his master. 'For so long I have envied your ability to move easily from one room to another.'

After some thought the master agreed, but warned him that Taoist magic could only be performed by someone with a pure heart and without evil intentions. Then he taught him what he wanted to know.

When the man arrived home, his wife was not at all impressed by what he had learned while he was away.

'I can't see any difference,' she grumbled. 'You might just as well have stayed here to help me for all the good it has done you.'

'Ah, but I have magic powers, now,' he retorted.

'I'll believe that when I see it,' she said. 'Come on now, show me your magic. What can you do?'

'I can walk through the wall,' said her husband, thinking that this was a good opportunity to take a look at the rich neighbours who had moved in next door while he was away.

Choosing his wall with care and concentrating hard, he walked straight towards it. Unfortunately he simply bumped his head hard against the wall, and his wife laughed as she helped him to his feet and a large lump began to swell on his forehead. With her laughter ringing in his ears, he was filled with embarrassment and shame, for he knew he had failed because his intentions had not been entirely pure.

Taoists of this kind were also very concerned to increase their life span and, if possible, to become immortal. They believed that it was possible to prolong life by the use of magic, and the necessary knowledge was eagerly sought after by many people, especially the emperors, who were rich enough to buy the most expensive ingredients for any form of drug. They were quite willing to spend a fortune in an effort to discover the elixir of everlasting life and no doubt many of them were cheated by dishonest Taoist masters who had no real knowledge of any drugs at all. Ironically many of the people who sought immortality died unpleasant deaths from taking drugs in the form of cinnabar, which contained the poisonous metal mercury. One legend tells of how, in the third century BC, the first Emperor of Chin sent a ship full of young boys and girls to the East with a Taoist master to seek for a magic herb which bestowed immortality. They did not find the herb but they never returned to China, preferring to colonize an island which later became the kingdom of Japan.

One of the founders of the magical Taoist religion was called Zhang Daoling. He was one of the leaders of a group of Taoist rebels called the Yellow Turbans who rose against the government in the second century AD. He achieved a

considerable following in the land of Shu, the present-day province of Sichuan, where he converted the people to his own form of Taoism. Although he was a true, historical person, Chinese folklore has built up many colourful and fantastic legends around him.

According to the legends, Zhang Daoling made a thorough study of the ways of achieving immortality. He succeeded in learning how to create the elixir of life, but he could not afford all the very expensive ingredients and he decided that he must find a way of making money. First of all he tried farming, but he soon found that that did not pay well. Next, having heard that the men of Shu were honest and hardworking and that Shu had many high mountains where he could communicate more closely with the immortals, he made his way there with his disciples. There he wrote a book about the Taoist Way, which explained some of the mysteries of Taoism and taught people the means of achieving immortality.

One day hundreds of immortals came down from the sky and taught Zhang further mysteries of the Way, including how to cure many diseases. People flocked to him from all around and there were soon so many thousands that something had to be done to look after them. Zhang proved as good at administration as he was at magic and in no time he had organized the people into a community. Each person contributed a tax of rice or some other useful food or object and some of the proceeds were shared among them all. Some, Zhang kept for his own use. Zhang also organized the building of roads and cesspools and generally improved the standard of life in the area. With his magic powers he was even able to punish those who failed to make their contribution: he made anyone trying to avoid doing their fair share of work fall ill—and few were prepared to run the risk of incurring Zhang's displeasure.

The community was so well run that some people even believed that the rules and regulations came from Heaven and they were therefore even more anxious to obey them. In this way Zhang amassed great wealth, until at last he was able to afford the ingredients to make the elixir. He made the elixir successfully but ate only half of it as he wished to stay amongst the people to convert more of them to Taoism. Half of the elixir was enough to give him the ability to perform even greater feats of magic, such as dividing himself into many parts. While one part of him was busy dealing with his disciples, the community or his guests, another part could be enjoying himself in a boat on the lake.

One of Zhang's favoured disciples was a young man called Zhao Sheng. He had been admitted to the inner circle of followers after being subjected to seven severe tests of his virtue and his

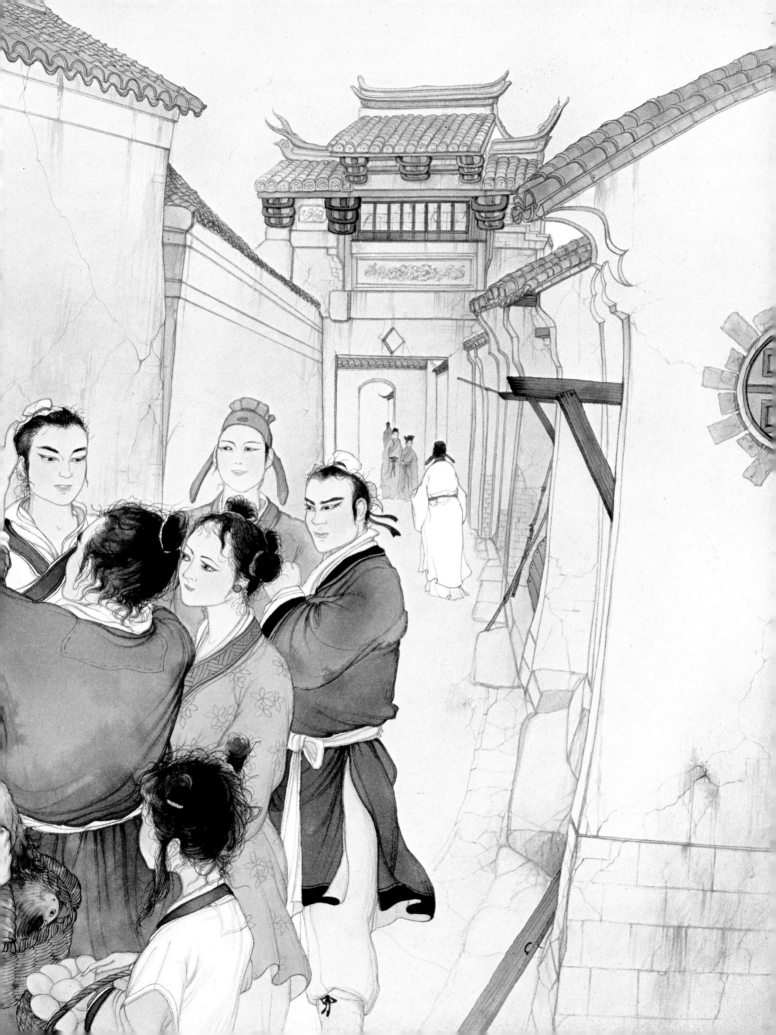

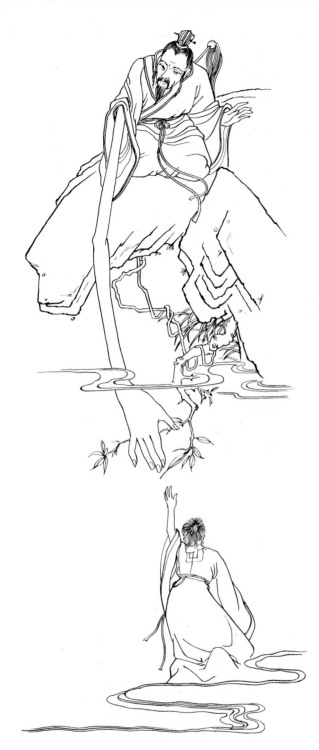

commitment to Taoism. The first test began as soon as he arrived. Instead of being welcomed, he was met with curses and laughter intended to humiliate him, but he stood fast and was not diverted from his intention to become Zhang's disciple. Another test was a trial of his chastity. He was ordered to watch the crops at night and as he did so, a beautiful girl approached him and asked to share his bed. Zhao allowed her to stay, but he did not touch her. Another of the tests concerned honesty. Casks of gold were placed beside a deserted road where he was walking, but he took nothing that did not belong to him. For the final test Zhang led his disciples to a steep cliff and pointed to a peach tree that was growing halfway down the cliff face. Then he said to the disciples, 'Anyone who fetches the peaches from the tree will achieve immortality.'

The cliff was so high and so steep that all the disciples were afraid to climb down to the peach tree but Zhao was not alarmed.
'If the immortal master protects, me, what do I have to fear?' he thought and immediately jumped over the edge of the cliff and landed safely in the tree. He threw the peaches up one by one and Zhang caught them and passed them on to the disciples, keeping one for Zhao.

Climbing back up the cliff was more difficult and Zhao found himself clinging helplessly to the sheer rock, unable to move upwards and not daring to look down to see how far below the ground lay. Seeing his difficulties, Zhang put his arm over the cliff edge and, as the disciples watched, the arm grew longer and longer until it reached Zhao and pulled him up to safety.

When they had eaten all the peaches, Zhang said that he would fetch some more and jumped over the cliff himself. Instead of landing in the tree, however, he fell right to the bottom of the cliff. The disciples lay on their stomachs and peered down at the tiny figure far below. Only Zhao and another favoured disciple did not hesitate. They followed their master over the cliff, landed safely and found Zhang waiting for them, laughing at the other disciples' lack of faith. Leaving the others still discussing their next move, Zhang and the two disciples ascended into Heaven to join the immortals, and were never seen again.

The eight immortals

In the thirteenth century during the Yüan dynasty, there appeared in popular folklore a group of eight Taoist deities who were known as the Eight Immortals. They were based partly on historical people and partly on imaginary characters, and at least one of them, Lü Dongbin, had featured in earlier Taoist tales. Now they were presented as a company—perhaps because the number eight was a favourite number of the Chinese. Their different personalities were also seen as representations of different types of people, the young and the old, the rich and the poor, the nobleman and the beggar, men and women. They often appeared in paintings together or singly, and were depicted as statuettes, painted on porcelain and lacquerware and used as decorations on all kinds of utensils; each immortal even had his or her own emblem by which he can be identified. The Chinese regarded them with affection and loved their eccentricities.

The first of the eight immortals is Li Tieguai, and he is one of the most famous of the group. His name means Li the Iron Crutch, and his emblem is a crutch and a gourd in which he carried medicine. Li became a proficient Taoist whose spirit was able to leave his body and go wandering all over the universe. On one such trip Li gave strict instructions to one of his disciples that he should guard his body well for at least seven days. If he had not returned by then, the guard might have the body cremated. The guard followed his orders and watched over the body most carefully, but on the sixth day he was summoned urgently to his mother's deathbed. Torn between the two duties, the guard finally decided to cremate the body (which looked quite dead) and go to his mother.

Li returned on the seventh day to find his body turned to ashes and his disconsolate spirit was forced to wander about with nowhere to stay. It happened that a one-legged beggar had died in nearby woods that same day and, to his disgust, Li had no alternative but to inhabit his filthy,

crippled body. The gods gave him a gold band to keep his dishevelled hair in place and an iron crutch to help him to move about. Despite his appearance, Li went to find the disciple who had burned his body and instead of scolding him, brought his dead mother back to life with some medicine from his gourd.

Li spent the rest of his life wandering from place to place, converting people to Taoism when he could. At night he would hang up his gourd and, shrinking into it, use it for shelter. Once he came across a man whom he thought he might be able to convert to the Taoist way of life. As a test, Li asked the man to follow him through a lighted furnace but the man did not have enough faith to try. Li then placed a leaf on a pool of water and asked the man to step on it but he was still too fearful and again refused. At this Li sighed, stepped onto the leaf himself and disappeared.

The second of the eight immortals is Han Zhongli, who is shown as an old man with a feather fan. It is said that he was once a marshal of the empire who later became a hermit and learned the way of immortality. Others say he was a Taoist priest who changed base metals into gold and silver by alchemy, using the riches he made to save people's lives during a famine.

One of Han Zhongli's converts was called Lü Dongbin and he, too, became one of the eight immortals. The character of Lü was based on a ninth century man who passed his public examinations at the advanced age of sixty-four. After his conversion to Taoism he travelled about the country performing minor miracles and helping the deserving. Once he came to a place where builders were working and had run out of food. He created a shoal of fishes in a lake for the hungry workers to catch and eat. On another occasion he found an old woman who was scrupulously honest in all her dealings and as a reward he turned the water in her well into wine. Lü is always shown carrying a sword with which to ward off evil demons and a fly whisk in the shape of a horse's tail.

The fourth and fifth members of the eight immortals are Zhang Guolao and Tsao Guojiu, also both old men. Zhang was always found riding a white donkey, a donkey which he was able to fold up and put away in his bag like a piece of paper when he did not need it. He was based on a holy man who lived in the eighth century. Tsao Guojiu, whose name means 'Uncle of the Emperor' was in fact the uncle of an empress in the eleventh century. Tsao had a disreputable younger brother who murdered an honest citizen and seduced his wife. The murdered man's ghost appeared to a fearless and incorruptible Judge named Bao and he immediately had Tsao's brother arrested. In order to protect his brother, Tsao tried to kill the wife but she was saved by a Taoist and went to complain to the judge herself. As a result the judge sent both brothers to prison.

The Empress pleaded with her husband to help her uncles and eventually the Emperor granted a general amnesty throughout the land and the two brothers were released. Tsao was so grateful that he renounced his worldly life and devoted himself completely to Taoism. He is usually shown in court robes, carrying the kind of polished wooden tablet that was normally used during an audience with the Emperor.

The sixth and seventh members are usually shown as young men. One is Han Shiangzi, who was the nephew of a ninth century poet and is shown carrying either flowers or peaches. According to the legend, he died falling out of a peach tree but came miraculously back to life again. The other young immortal is Lan Tsaiho, an actor and singer who used to sing in the streets about the unimportance of earthly life, urging people to become Taoists.

The last of the eight immortals, and the only woman in the company, is Ho Shiangu, who is shown carrying a lotus. She was a young girl who lost her way in the mountains and was saved when Lü Dongbin appeared, gave her a peach and showed her the way home. When she had eaten the peach she received the gift of prophecy and, later, of immortality.

Chinese people loved the eight immortals but they did not take them very seriously, treating them more as we treat a character like Father Christmas than as religious figures. It is certainly reassuring to imagine them wandering about the world, sometimes alone, sometimes together, rejecting the values of earthbound humans and now and again giving people in trouble a helping hand with their magic powers.

Spirits and demons

In the old days the Chinese people believed that animals could assume human form and live among people undetected. Many of these strange animals used their magic powers to enable them to live to a tremendous age—some even for centuries. Often they had evil intentions towards human beings and even if they were not evil they were always considered unnatural and were regarded with disgust, especially when they took on human form. Sometimes even inanimate objects contained evil spirits which could assume different shapes and cause misfortune and illness to human beings. When animal or other spirits were discovered in their unnatural forms, they were usually treated harshly and exorcized as if they were some kind of ghost or demon.

To be possessed by spirit demons was very similar to being haunted by ghosts. Like ghosts, the spirits generally shunned the daylight and would suddenly appear and disappear. In most cases exorcism forced the spirit demon to return to its original form, when it apparently lost its magic powers and could be captured and killed like any normal member of its species.

Many of the stories about spirits and demons were popular variations on the ghost story theme, told to a trembling audience as they gathered round the flickering lamplight. Like ghost stories they must have seemed more than half real, especially in the thick darkness and silence of the countryside. It would have been easy enough to imagine yourself in the same situation as the man from Hejian whose story follows.

There was once a well-to-do man who lived at Hejian in nothern China. In his yard there was a huge stack of straw and every day the servants took some straw out of it to use in the household. Before very long there was a big hole in the side of the stack and a fox decided to make this his home. One day the fox came up to the master of the house in the form of an old man and invited him to have a drink with him in his hole. At first the man refused but in the end he allowed himself to be persuaded and, bending down, he crawled through the dusty hole into the stack of straw.

To the man's astonishment, he found that inside the hole there was a succession of luxuriously furnished rooms, each richer and more comfortable than the last. The fox and the man sat down and servants brought them tea and wine to drink. It was so dark inside the room that the man could not tell whether it was day or night and he stayed a long time, chatting to the fox in a friendly way. After a time they finished and before the man's astonished eyes, all the cups, wine jars and tea-making equipment vanished into nothing.

Although he was surprised, the man was enjoying the fox's company and he decided to ask him a question that had been puzzling him for some time. All the time the fox had been living in the stack, he had always disappeared at night. During the hours of darkness no-one ever saw him and only at dawn did he come trotting back into the yard. No-one had been able to follow him to find out where he went. Now the man took his chance to ask him about it.

'Friends invite me to come for a drink,' replied the fox.

'May I come with you?' asked the man.

At first the fox said this was not possible, but when the man begged him again and again, he finally agreed.

'Hold tight,' said the fox and, taking the man by the arm, he tugged him off the ground. They seemed to travel through the air like the wind and before long they arrived at a city the man had never seen before. The fox led the way to a wine shop where a group of people were enjoying a feast. Still holding the man by the arm, he took him up some stairs to a small landing where they could look down on the people below and see the different foods that were being offered. Soon the fox went down, helped himself to food and drink and came back to join the man on the landing. The people in the wine shop did nothing to prevent him, so the man gratefully accepted his plateful of food.

While they were eating and drinking, the man noticed a plate of cumquats, delicious miniature oranges, on one of the tables. They were in front of a man wearing a red coat.

'Could you fetch me some of that fruit?' he asked the fox.

'No, I cannot,' replied the fox. 'That is a man who is beyond reproach. I cannot go near him.'

At this the man was silent. 'If the fox cannot go near a good man, what does that make me?' he thought to himself. 'He had no hesitation in

approaching me—why we have even eaten and drunk together.' There and then he decided to try to live a better life and have nothing more to do with these exciting but dangerous spirits.

The decision was barely formed in his mind when he felt himself losing his balance and falling head over heels down the stairs. He landed with a thump among the group below.

The people seemed quite astonished to find a stranger suddenly among them and when the man looked up he saw the reason for their surprise: there was no flight of stairs and no landing above the room. He and the fox had been perched on a beam in the roof and had apparently been unnoticed by the crowd.

At first the people thought they were being haunted and were ready to attack the man as an evil spirit but he told them what had happened and they believed his strange story. When he asked them where he was he was told that he was at a place called Yütai in the Shandong Peninsula, about a thousand *li* away from home. (One *li* is equal to a third of a mile.)

The guests at the party all collected some money and helped to send him home to Hejian. As for the fox, wherever he went, he never returned to the stack of straw.

The haunted pavilion

In the old days, when travellers often spent many days and nights on a journey, it was the custom to provide resting places and shelters along the roads. In these shelters, or pavilions, the travellers could sleep and buy a meal from the people who looked after the building.

Some time during the third century, just south of the city of Anyang, there was a pavilion where no-one dared to stay the night: it was haunted. Anyone who was foolish enough to stay there was found dead next morning, unmarked but with the signs of terrible agony on his face.

One night a young scholar arrived at the pavilion, hoping for a night's lodging before continuing his journey south. The people who looked after the place warned him that it would not be safe for him to spend the night there but the scholar was well trained in the magic arts and would not be deterred.

'I believe I know how to look after myself,' he said confidently. 'And it's time someone cleared this mystery up.'

Muttering to themselves, the people left him food and drink and, since they dared not stay at the pavilion themselves, they hurried back to their homes. Darkness fell and the scholar settled down in one of the rooms and began to read aloud from his books.

He went on reading for a long time until in the dead of night he heard soft footsteps outside and, looking out, saw someone dressed all in black approaching the front of the pavilion. Suddenly a voice called out: 'Pavilion master!'

Another voice answered, 'Here I am, what do you want?'

The man in black said, 'I see there is someone in the pavilion.'

'Yes,' replied the second voice, 'a scholar is here reading his books, but he is not yet asleep.' The figure in black sighed and went away.

The scholar returned to his reading and after a while a figure wearing a red hat approached. 'Pavilion master!' cried a strong voice.

'Here I am, what do you want?' answered the voice of the pavilion master.

'I see there is someone in the pavilion.'

'Yes, a scholar is here reading his books, but he is not yet asleep.'

Like the first visitor, the figure in the red hat sighed deeply and went away. The scholar waited for a short while and then crept to the front of the pavilion, where he too called out, 'Pavilion master!'

The voice replied, 'Here I am, what do you want?'

'I see there is someone in the pavilion.'

'Yes,' said the voice, 'a scholar is here reading his books, but he is not yet asleep.' The scholar sighed as the others had done, and then he asked, 'Who was the man in black?'

The voice replied, 'That was the black sow from the North house.'

'And who was the man in the red hat?'

'That was the old cock from the West house.'

Then the scholar asked, 'And who are you?'

'I am an aged scorpion,' replied the voice.

The scholar crept back into the pavilion and went on reading aloud from his books, but he did not dare fall asleep. At dawn the people who looked after the pavilion came back and were surprised to see him alive and well.

'How did you manage to stay alive?' one of them asked. The scholar did not answer the question but said firmly, 'Bring me a sword and I will rid you of your demons. From this day on, no traveller will die in this pavilion.'

One of the men ran to fetch a sword and the scholar led them to a corner of the pavilion where the voice of the pavilion master had seemed to come from. There, hidden in a crack in the wall, he found a huge scorpion, its great claws open to attack and its stinging tail curled angrily over its back. The scholar thrust the sword deep into the scorpion's body and killed it instantly. Next he asked the people to lead him to the North house where he found an old black sow rooting about among the grass. To the people's surprise he killed this also. Finally they showed him the West house, where he found an old cock with a large red crest: without a word he cut its head right off.

The scholar explained how he had discovered who the demons were and, as he had promised, from that day on, travellers were able to spend the night safely in the pavilion and continue on their journey refreshed.

The night bird

There was once a man of Chu in central China by the name of Li, who was a huntsman and a man of good character. Whenever Li went hunting he always came back with a good catch and he and his family managed to live well. Nearby there lived a wealthy man called Dong. Dong's family was prosperous, living in a large house with many rooms around a courtyard. Unfortunately, Dong's mother suffered from a terrible illness. During the day she was always perfectly fit and healthy but at night she was attacked by unbearable pains. She felt as if her back was being stabbed over and over again with a sharp knife and as if her arms and legs were being beaten black and blue. In the morning, however, there was no sign of any injury. She had suffered in this way for a year but neither medicines nor acupunture seemed able to cure her.

One day a wise and famous diviner passed through the district and stayed at Dong's house for the night. As usual, Dong's mother screamed out with pain in the middle of the night as if she were being tortured and next morning the diviner asked Dong: 'What illness does your mother suffer from that she screams in such torment?'

Dong could only reply, 'We do not know the cause of her illness and nothing can cure it. My mother has suffered like this for a whole year and I am afraid that if the torment continues she will no longer have the strength to live.'

When he heard this, the wise man used his powers of divination to discover the cause of the illness and said to Dong, 'Today you will meet a man with a bow by the roadside. You must prepare gifts of clothing and invite him to stay here for the night, for he will discover the cause of your mother's illness and be able to cure it.' Having told him this, the diviner went on his way.

Dong did as the diviner had said; he prepared gifts of clothing and waited at the roadside. After some time Li the huntsman came along with his bow and arrow. Dong greeted Li and begged him to stay at his house for the night. But Li answered, 'I am a huntsman and I have not shot anything yet today. Why are you stopping me like this? It is still early and I cannot stop work now.'

Dong explained courteously, 'My mother's suffering is more than she can bear and a wise man told me that if I could keep you in my house for one night, she would be cured. Please come as my guest and I will give you food and drink that will more than make up for your lost hunting time.'

Li agreed to help and together they returned to Dong's house. Li was given a feast of food and drink and, as night fell, was shown to a room on the east side of the house.

That night the moon was very bright and Li, being unable to sleep, strolled about the house and courtyard for some time. Suddenly he saw a huge bird come down from the sky and start to peck at the door to Dong's mother's room. At the same time he heard groans and screams coming from inside. Li suspected at once that the bird might be a spirit demon, and he hurried back to his room to get his bow and arrows. When he returned, the bird was still there and Li quickly shot it with several arrows. The bird disappeared and the noise inside the room stopped.

Next morning Li said to Dong, 'I think I have destroyed the cause of your mother's illness.' 'How did you do it?' asked Dong. 'Last night at about midnight I was walking in the courtyard when suddenly I saw a huge bird, all red in colour, with two eyes like points of gold. It flew straight to the house and pecked at the door of your mother's room. I heard her groan inside so I took my bow and arrow and shot it again and again. Ask your mother how she feels this morning. For as soon as the bird disappeared, she fell silent.'

Dong was very pleased and went off to search for traces of the bird. At first he could find nothing but then, in the corner of the kitchen, he saw a large wooden pestle which was used for pounding grain into fine meal. Two long arrows were sticking into its side and there were traces of blood where the arrows had struck their mark.

'Aha,' cried Dong, 'so it is your spirit, pestle, which has been causing my mother so much pain. I'll soon put a stop to that.' And he seized the pestle and threw it onto the fire, waiting to make sure that it burned completely away before scattering the white ashes in the wind.

So the demon of the pestle was destroyed and Dong's mother was completely cured.

Lady White

The city of Hangzhou stands on the shores of the most beautiful lake in China, West Lake. Though not very large overall, the lake is wide enough to give a sense of a large expanse of water and is made more beautiful by the low-lying hills which surround it. Wonderful pavilions and pagodas are to be found nestling amongst the hills, presenting a beautiful view wherever one looks. The city itself has always been an important commercial centre, renowned for its silk, embroidery and tea. This combination of city and lake have attracted artists and tourists through the centuries and they provide an appropriate setting for the following legend, one of the best loved romances of China.

There was once a young man in his early twenties named Shüshuan. He had been an orphan since childhood and lived with his sister and her family in Hangzhou where he worked in his uncle's shop. One spring during the Festival of the Dead, which was called the Festival of Bright and Clear, he went to a temple situated on the other side of the lake to burn incense and offer sacrifices to the souls of his dead parents. When the ceremony was over, he walked along the shores of the lake enjoying the spring sunshine.

Quite suddenly it started to rain and Shüshuan looked around for a boat to ferry him across the lake to Hangzhou. He soon found one and just as the boat was pulling away from the shore, someone else shouted to be ferried across the lake. Shüshuan turned to see who it was and saw a young woman dressed totally in white as if in mourning, white being the colour of mourning in China. Another young girl dressed in blue, who appeared to be her maid, was standing beside her.

The ferryman returned to the shore and soon the two young women were seated in the boat with Shüshuan. He saw that the woman in white was very beautiful and that although she was dressed in mourning, her clothes were very expensive. She smiled gently at him and he felt flattered at her attention. They soon fell into conversation and after Shüshuan had told her all about himself, he asked her name.
'My name is White,' she said. 'I was recently widowed and as today is the Festival of the Dead,

I have been to tend my husband's grave and offer sacrifices to his soul. I left in such a hurry this morning that I have forgotten to bring any money with me; I have not even enough to pay the ferryman. Would you be kind enough, sir, to pay him on my behalf? When you have time, you could then come to my house so that I can repay you. I live in Hangzhou, near Arrow Bridge.'

Shüshuan was only too willing to help and paid the ferryman when they reached the other side of the lake. It was still raining and as Shüshuan had an umbrella, he offered to walk part of the way home with her. In the end he lent her the umbrella, saying that he would be happy to come to her house to fetch it next day.

That night he could not sleep and as he tossed and turned in the darkness, his mind kept wandering towards the woman in white. The following day he asked to have the afternoon off from the shop and went straight to Arrow Bridge. He asked people who lived in the area, but no-one seemed to know who the young widow was or where she lived. Fortunately, he caught sight of the maid, who was out on an errand for her mistress and she led him to a large house nearby. The lady received him in a beautifully decorated room, offering him food and wine. She spoke to him shyly but directly, and after a while told him that she felt a great affection for him. 'Our meeting on the ferry was destined to happen,' she said. 'I hope that you, too, have some affection for me and that you will be willing to marry me.' Shüshuan was overwhelmed with delight, but he remained silent, for he did not see how he could possibly marry her when he had no property of his own and lived as a lodger with his sister.

'Will you give me no answer?' asked Lady White. Shüshuan confessed his poverty, to which she replied, 'A problem such as that is easily solved!' She asked her maid to fetch fifty pieces of silver and gave these to him wrapped in a white cloth. She assured him that there was plenty more if he should have need of it and Shüshuan took the silver, promising to return soon.

On his way home he bought a cooked chicken, and a goose, as well as many accompanying dishes and a large bottle of wine. When he arrived back at his sister's house, he invited her and her husband to join him in the feast. They were surprised that he had been able to afford so much food and waited for an explanation. Eventually he broached the subject of his forthcoming marriage and brought out the pieces of silver which Lady White had given him. His brother-in-law took the silver and examined it carefully. Then he suddenly cried, 'This is terrible! We shall all be ruined!' He pointed with a trembling hand to the small mark stamped on each piece of silver. 'That is the mark of the official treasury,' he cried. 'This silver must have been stolen. It was announced only a few days ago that thieves had broken into the treasury and there is a warrant out for their arrest. They are offering a reward for information and anyone harbouring the thieves will be severely punished!' He quickly wrapped up the silver and rushed off to the magistrate, who immediately sent his men to arrest Shüshuan on a charge of robbery.

Shüshuan was terrified and told the magistrate how he had come by the silver. The police went straightaway to the house near Arrow Bridge, but found it locked and seemingly deserted. The neighbours said that the house was empty, but haunted. The last family to live there had all died mysteriously, and strange movements had been seen after dark in the house. After these eerie stories the men were reluctant to enter but at last they plucked up courage to break down the door and go inside.

It was dark in the house after the bright sunlight and for a moment the men could see nothing. Then, at the top of the stairs they saw a woman standing, dressed all in white. One of the men was about to strike her when there was a crash of thunder and she disappeared. In the place where she had been standing was a pile of silver pieces.

The silver pieces were easily identified as the remainder of the stolen hoard and Shüshuan was set free. However, because he had been involved in the strange affair, he was banished from the city.

Through the kindness of his friends, Shüshuan found a job in the neighbouring city of Suzhou and he moved to live there. After six months had passed he was reconciled to his life once more. Then one day he was sitting at home when a closed sedan chair came to the house and he was

called for. To his horror he found that the sedan chair contained Lady White, and that her little maid was standing behind it.

'Thief, demon,' shouted Shüshuan when he saw her, but she only smiled gently at him and asked to speak to him in private.

'It was all a terrible mistake,' she explained when they were alone inside. 'Whatever made you think I was a thief? Look at me. How can you believe that I am a demon? The silver was left to me by my former husband and I have absolutely no idea where he got it from. I was quite terrified when I heard that you had been arrested, and I persuaded my neighbours to tell the story about the house being haunted. I was just putting the silver in a pile when the police burst in and saw me. I was so frightened that I simply ran away. The men were already so scared by the neighbours' ghostly stories that their imaginations did all the rest. It has taken me six months to find out what happened to you. Please forgive me for all the trouble which I have caused you. I have brought more money so that we can be married and live together as man and wife.'

She spoke so convincingly that Shüshuan felt all his hostility and anger melting away. She quickly made friends with his landlord and his wife, and they helped her to persuade Shüshuan to forgive her. He found it very hard to resist them all and before long he and Lady White were married.

They were extremely happy together and Shüshuan's wife looked after him very well. Thanks to her wealth, he was able to do as he wished and live in relative comfort. About a year after the wedding, there was a big religious festival at a temple outside the city and Shüshuan's friends invited him to join them there. His wife was reluctant to let him go, but she finally agreed if he promised her three things: firstly, he must not speak to any monk or priest; secondly, he must not enter the temple itself, but only join in the festivities outside; and thirdly, he must not stay out late. He agreed to these three conditions and went off to enjoy himself with his friends.

For some time they were content to try all the amusements outside the temple, but after a while Shüshuan's friends decided to go inside the building to have a look around.

'I promised my wife faithfully that I would not step inside the temple,' said Shüshuan.

'Don't worry,' they replied. 'She'll never know! We won't tell.' And so he went with them.

Inside the temple there were many monks and priests praying and worshipping, and amongst them was a highly respected priest of exceptional piety called Master Fahai. As soon as he saw Shüshuan, he called out, 'Bring that man to me. I must speak with him!' But Shüshuan had already gone out of the temple and before anyone could reach him he was well on his way home. He was just approaching the bank of a river near the temple when he saw a boat almost flying over the water towards him. To his surprise he saw his wife and her maid leaning out of it, beckoning to him anxiously.

'Quick, Shüshuan,' called his wife, 'jump in here with us.'

Shüshuan looked over his shoulder to see what could be the matter and at that moment Master Fahai caught up with him. Master Fahai, too, saw the women in the boat and he held out his hands and cursed them.

'Begone, demons, and do not trouble this young man again!' he cried in a terrible voice.

The two women recoiled in terror, the boat rocked violently, overturned and the women sank into the river without a trace.

Master Fahai turned to Shüshuan and said, 'I knew at once that you were under the spell of a powerful demon. Now I have sent her away. If she ever returns to pester you again, tell me and I will deal with her.' Shüshuan was very shaken by these events and when the Emperor granted a general amnesty to all those in exile, he quickly packed his belongings and returned to Hangzhou.

When he arrived at his sister's house, she and her husband greeted him with affection, but said reproachfully, 'Why didn't you let us know you were coming? And you might have told us that you were married. We would have liked to celebrate the wedding. Still, your wife is here already, so we can celebrate tonight.' And there was Lady White, sitting with his sister just like one of the family. Shüshuan was about to protest but Lady White looked at him in a way she had never done before and he remained silent. When they were alone she said, 'Although I treated you with all my love and consideration, and although we were so happy together, you still chose to believe the words of some meddling priest. You ungrateful wretch! Now you know my powers, beware. One disobedient word from you again, and I shall turn Hangzhou into a blood bath!' Shüshuan was terrified and could only mumble that he thought she had been drowned in the river. Frightened of his wife and at the same afraid for his sister and her family, he decided that it was best to pretend that all was well.

Next day he went out of the house, too miserable to do anything else. The only help he could think of was Master Fahai, and he was miles away in Suzhou. He walked towards the lake and stood there gloomily, wondering if he should put an end to all his troubles by drowning himself. As he stood there, he heard a quiet voice say, 'How can a man have such little regard for life? If you have troubles, let me help you.' Shüshuan turned to find Master Fahai standing there. When he heard what had happened in Hangzhou, the Master gave Shüshuan his monk's begging bowl. 'Do not be afraid,' he said. 'Take this bowl and when the woman is not looking, clap it on top of her head and press down hard. Keep on pressing down until the bowl reaches the floor. I will be there to help.'

With the bowl hidden under his clothes, Shüshuan returned home where he found Lady White sitting trembling with rage because he had gone out without her knowledge. He crept up quietly behind her and before she could turn round, placed the bowl on her head and pressed it down as hard as he could. As he pressed he felt her shrinking under his weight and then he heard her voice, now low and pleading, 'Husband, husband, do not do this to me. Remember our love. Remember our life together.' But Shüshuan was deaf to her pleas and pressed the bowl down and down until it rested on the ground.

At that moment Master Fahai was shown in and, placing his hand lightly on the bowl he said: 'Show your true form, demon. Who are you?'

A voice from beneath the bowl answered: 'I am a white python, many centuries old. The movement of wind and tides brought me to come and live at West Lake and I made friends with an

ancient blue fish who became my faithful maid. When I saw Shüshuan I could not stop myself from falling in love with him. I have not harmed him, have I? Please take pity on me!'

Master Fahai chanted some spells and then turned the bowl over. There inside was a tiny white snake, coil upon coil, and a small blue fish. He covered the bowl and took it outside the city, where he ordered the local citizens to build a tall pagoda packed with holy relics and to place the sealed bowl in its foundations.

'So long as the pagoda stands,' he said, 'the two demons will be imprisoned beneath it.' When the pagoda had been built, Shüshuan became a monk and followed Master Fahai.

The pagoda stood for many centuries on the shore of the West Lake but collapsed in 1934 for lack of proper maintenance. No-one noticed a small white python or a blue fish wriggling out of the rubble and into the water—but perhaps no-one was looking at the time.

The story of Lady Ren

During the time of the Tang dynasty there lived a man called Zheng. He was one of a group of struggling young men who thronged the rich, cosmopolitan capital of China—at that time a city named Chang'an in the central eastern region.

One summer evening Zheng was riding on his donkey to a place just outside the city wall where he had arranged to meet some friends before going off on a drinking spree. As he made his way through the crowd that was going out of the city gate, he saw a group of women in front of him, one of whom was outstandingly beautiful. Zheng was so amazed by the woman's beauty that he could not stop staring at her. He followed her for a while and sometimes rode a few paces ahead of her, but he did not take his eyes off her for a moment.

Zheng's behaviour did not go unnoticed and as he thought he detected a sympathetic look in the girl's eye, he spoke up.

'Why is it that a pretty girl like you is walking and not riding?' he asked.

'When someone with a mount fails to offer it,

what else can a girl do?' replied the girl quickly, smiling at him.

'My donkey is not nearly good enough for someone as pretty as you,' said Zheng, 'but I would give him up straight away if I could come along with you.'

So they went on talking and teasing one another until they had left the city quite a long way behind. It was dark by now and Zheng could not see where they were going but before long they came to a house with a most imposing gateway. The girl invited Zheng to follow her inside and there they were greeted and waited on by many servants. The girl said her name was Ren and encouraged him to stay, so, having eaten and drunk his fill, he spent the night with her. Before daylight, she woke him.

'You must go now,' she whispered, 'for my brothers will be very angry if they find you here.'

They arranged to meet again and Zheng made his way back to the city. When he arrived at the city gate, he found it was still closed and he settled down to wait along with all the other early risers. He bought something to eat and drink from a Turkish stall keeper who had just lit his stove and hung up some lanterns and they fell into conversation. Zheng, nodding in the direction from which he had come, asked him: 'If you turn to the east from here, there is a house with a big gateway. Do you know whose house it is?'

The stall keeper said, 'It's just desolate wasteland out there. There are no houses.'

'Yes there are,' said Zheng, 'I've just been to one of them!' and started to argue with him.

The stall keeper looked puzzled, and then realization dawned and he said, 'Now I remember. A fox spirit lives there, who often entices men to spend the night with her. I've met three of her victims already. Now you're the fourth.'

'No, no, you must be mistaken,' said Zheng, trying to hide his dismay, but now that it was light he went back to have a look, and indeed there was only a piece of wasteland where the house had stood, behind the ruins of a gate. He returned sadly to the city but he soon found that, try as he might, he could not keep his mind off his encounter with the girl called Ren.

A week later he saw Ren again in the street

going into a clothes shop and, calling her, he made his way through the crowd towards her. But she hid her face behind her fan and did not want to speak to him. Very quietly she said, 'Now that you know the truth, why do you still come near me?'

'What if I do know?' asked Zheng. 'What difference does it make?'

'I am so ashamed,' replied Ren, 'I can hardly speak to you. I was afraid you would not want to have anything more to do with me.' Zheng swore that this was not the case and Ren continued, lowering her fan, 'People hate us because we are supposed to harm them, but I am not like that. If you do not think ill of me, I would like to be your wife and serve you for the rest of my life.' Zheng was delighted.

Zheng then set about looking for suitable accommodation. Ren gave him instructions. 'If you go in an easterly direction from here, you will soon see a large tree growing out of the wall of a house. It is a quiet street and there is a house to let which we can rent. Does not your brother-in-law Wei Yin have some furniture and cooking pots at his disposal, left with him by some relations? We can borrow them and that will save us some money.'

Zheng did as he was told and found the house just as Ren had described. Then he went to his brother-in-law, who also happened to be one of his closest friends, a wealthy and dissolute young man about town. Wei was curious about what was going on and, hearing of Ren's great beauty, was filled with wicked intentions. He secretly followed his friend to his new home and waited outside in the shadows until Zheng went out on business. Pushing his way in, he found Ren trying to hide behind the curtain and pulled her roughly to him, trying to kiss her. Ren resisted strongly. 'What are you trying to do?' she asked. 'Zheng may not be as handsome or as rich as you but he is an honest man and you are supposed to be his friend. He has only me in all the world while you, sir, have good looks, wealth and influence. You can have all the women you want; would you rob your friend of the only thing he values?'

Ren's words made Wei feel very ashamed and he let her go at once. After this they became good friends and they would often do each other favours, he with his money and she with her supernatural powers. She was a good wife to Zheng and looked after the household perfectly. The only thing she would not do was needlework and she never made any of her own clothes. 'Anyway, the ones in the shops are much better than any I could make,' she used to say.

With Ren's help, Zheng prospered and the pair lived happily together. Ren had ways of supplementing Zheng's meagre income. One day she asked him, 'Can you get together five thousand cash (copper coins)? I have a good use for it.' It was not a very big sum and Zheng borrowed it easily from his friends. With it, Ren told him to go to the market next day and buy a horse which had a certain mark on its left flank. At the market Zheng soon saw a man leading such a horse and he bought it at once. Zheng's friend Wei laughed at him and said, 'That horse is broken down, why spend money on it?' He took no notice and led it home to Ren.

A few days later Ren told Zheng, 'Now you can take it to the market and sell it for at least thirty thousand cash.' At the market a man came and offered Zheng twenty thousand cash, but he held out against it and went home with the horse at the end of the day. But the man followed him and finally offered him thirty thousand cash. In this way, after repaying his debt, he had a clear profit of twenty-five thousand cash. Everyone was astonished. It turned out that the man who had bought it had been given charge of an imperial horse with just such a mark on its flank. The horse had died three years earlier but the man had failed to report the death. Instead he had continued to claim for its keep and feed, which had been worth sixty thousand to him. Now the horse was being recalled for a muster and the man was desperate to find one with identical markings and was willing to forgo half of his illicit gains.

A few years later Zheng was asked to carry out a commission a long way from the capital. The business would take some time to complete and he knew that he would have to spend several weeks away from home. He was eager to take the commission which was important for his career and as he did not want to leave Ren for so long, he asked her to go with him. To his surprise she said firmly that she would prefer to stay in Chang'an and, unable to persuade her himself, he enlisted Wei's help. Even this was no use. Finally, when they had almost given up arguing with her, Ren admitted, 'I have heard that it would be unlucky for me to journey in that direction this year.

That's the real reason why I do not wish to go. I am afraid of what may happen.'

The two men laughed. 'Surely you of all people have nothing to fear,' said Zheng. 'You understand the spirits better than most people.'

The two of them scoffed at her, telling her it was all utter nonsense and pressing her to go as before. At last, because she could think of no other convincing arguments, Ren agreed to go with him. Wei lent them his horses and, followed by Ren's maid, they left the city.

All went well on their journey until they reached the mountains. As they rode along a narrow path, they could hear a large group of huntsmen and hounds nearby. Suddenly black hounds appeared from all directions and headed towards them. Zheng looked at Ren. To his horror he saw her start to shrivel up and turn back into a fox. The fox jumped down from the horse and ran as fast as she could, but she did not get very far before the hounds caught her. By the time Zheng had reached the spot, there was nothing left of his beloved Ren but the bloody corpse of a fox. Her clothes were left on the horse's saddle, looking like a chrysalis abandoned by a butterfly, her shoes were still in the stirrups, and her jewels were scattered over the ground. Her maid had disappeared.

Zheng retrieved the corpse from the hounds, giving some money to the huntsmen, and buried Ren in an honourable manner. When he returned to the capital, he went to share his grief with his friend Wei. Wei was horrified and said to him, 'Hunting hounds are fierce animals, but I have never heard of them killing a woman before.' 'But Ren was not a woman,' said Zheng. 'Not a woman?' cried Wei in amazement. 'What was she then?' Zheng then told his friend the complete story and together they wept and lamented her death.

Some time later they both made a pilgrimage to her grave and, when they recalled her life, she seemed to them no different from other women except that she had done no needlework. In all other respects she had been a perfect wife and a most virtuous woman. After this, Zheng's life continued to prosper and he lived to be an old man and to gain many honours. But he never forgot his beautiful spirit wife.

The god behind the curtain

In Shandong there was a man by the name of Liang Wen, who was a fervent Taoist believer. In his house he built a Taoist temple of some size. He put rich curtains around the altar and often worshipped before it.

After about ten years had passed, he was performing some sacrifice before the altar when suddenly a voice addressed him from behind the curtains. The voice claimed to belong to the God of Gaoshan and Liang hastened to place sacrificial meats and wines before it. It was soon obvious that the god had a voracious appetite for he ate and drank everything that was placed before him. However, he also seemed able to cure all kinds of illnesses and people began to visit the temple, which soon became very popular.

For seven or eight years this continued and Liang conducted himself with the utmost propriety and always showed the greatest humility when he was in the temple. In all these years he never went behind the curtains around the altar. One day, however, the god seemed to have had too much to drink and sounded quite intoxicated. Liang asked permission to wait on him behind the curtain.

'You may put your hand through the curtain,' said the god simply.

Liang did so and found himself touching the god's face, which seemed to have an extraordinarily long beard. As he felt all over the face he suddenly had an urge to give the beard a tug. To his surprise there was a loud 'baaing' sound, just like a goat. The people in the temple were astonished and together they helped Liang search behind the curtain.

The god turned out to be a goat which had wandered off from a neighbour's flock seven or eight years before. It was soon killed and eaten and the god never appeared in the temple again.

The bell-shaped pendant

Once there was a man whose surname was Wang who had to make a long journey away from home. He was travelling by boat and one evening as the boat was being moored for the night, Wang stepped ashore to look for an inn to stay the night. On the bank above the river he saw a beautiful young woman who looked about sixteen or seventeen years old. Seeing that she was alone, Wang hailed her and, after talking to her for a little while, asked her if she would spend the night with him. She agreed. The next morning he took off a golden, bell-shaped pendant he wore and tied it to her arm without her knowing.

When the girl left, Wang sent his servant to follow her and find out where she lived. The servant followed her secretly all the way into a house, but then she seemed to disappear. There were no women living in the house, he was told, and there was no way by which the girl could have left without the servant seeing her.

As they searched they happened to come right up against the pig sty. The servant looked inside and noticed to his astonishment that the sow was wearing a bell-shaped pendant on its front leg. Without another word, the servant ran from the house and he and his master left the town the same day, never to return.

The Monkey spirit

There was once a mountain called the Mountain of Flowers and Fruits which rose from the middle of the sea. On the top of the mountain was an unusual stone. It was gigantic in size and possessed special powers, for ever since Pangu had created the universe it had lain there receiving nourishment from the essences of the sky, the earth, the sun and the moon. One day the stone suddenly split and gave birth to a stone egg. As the elements played around it, the stone egg gradually turned into a Monkey. This Monkey, though of ordinary size, was no ordinary animal.

Monkey explored his surroundings, jumping and climbing around as any monkey might, eating wild fruits and drinking from the springs. His companions were the beasts of the mountains and forests; in particular he joined a tribe of wild monkeys, going wherever they went and doing whatever they did. Eventually he led them to a secure home in a cave behind a waterfall at the top of the Mountain of Flowers and Fruit and, with their consent, he became their king.

After the Stone Monkey had been a wise and well loved king to the monkeys for about three hundred years, he began to worry about the future. The other monkeys laughed at him and asked: 'How can we lead a more contented life than we already do, for we have all that we need in the way of food, drink and shelter?'
'Whatever we do here, we still have death to fear,' replied Monkey, 'for one day Lord Yama of the Underworld will claim us and we shall have to go.'
'O King,' said one monkey 'do you know about the Buddha, the deities and the immortals who need never die?'

Monkey was cheered to hear this. 'I will look for them and see if I, too, can learn the way of immortality,' he said.

The next day Monkey went down the mountain and crossed the sea in a raft to the world of men. After wandering about the world for a long time he found his way to a mountain where a woodcutter showed him a path to a cave high up the mountainside. There lived a holy man called Master Subodhi, who taught the way to eternal life. Monkey found the cave but there was a wooden door across the entrance and it was shut fast. Monkey felt too shy to knock on the door; instead he climbed up a pine tree just outside and sat nibbling pine kernels. In a little while the door opened and a page boy looked out saying, 'Who is that out here making such a noise?'

Monkey hastily slid down the tree trunk and made a bow to the page. 'Sir page, I have come to be a disciple to your master. I wouldn't dare to make a noise here.'

'Are you a seeker after the Way?' asked the page.

'Yes,' said Monkey.

'How strange,' said the page. 'The Master was about to interpret the scriptures when suddenly he looked up and turned to me saying that I must go to the door and let in whoever comes to seek after the Way. I expect he meant you. You had better come in.'

Monkey was led before the learned Master. 'Where do you come from?' asked the Master.

'From the Mountain of Flowers and Fruit.'

'Be off with you; what a liar!' said the Master angrily. 'How can you have come from there when there is the sea to cross, to say nothing of all the land between there and here.'

Monkey protested that he had told the truth and recounted the story of his birth from the stone egg. Realizing that this was no ordinary monkey, Master Subodhi accepted him as a disciple and gave him a new name, as was the custom for those who left their homes to follow a Master and learn the Way. The Monkey's name was Sun the Enlightened One, *sun* being one of the Chinese words for monkey.

Havoc in Heaven

Monkey spent twenty years with Master Subodhi learning the way of eternal life. The Master also taught him many other skills, such as how to turn 'cloud somersaults', great whirling somersaults through the air that carried him several thousand *li*, and also how to change himself into any shape. When he returned to the Mountain of Flowers and Fruit he found a demon monster had taken possession of the monkey tribe's Curtain Cave behind the waterfall and his first task was to fight and vanquish it so that the monkeys could live happily there once more. After the fight he realized that he needed a good weapon, so he visited the Dragon King of the Eastern Sea and, against the dragon's will, took away a magic iron pillar which had been used as a post by the flood controller, Yü. This pillar could be changed to any size its owner needed so that it could be a staff eight feet long for fighting hand to hand, or could shrink to the size of an embroidery needle to be carried behind Monkey's ear.

Monkey returned with the pillar to his home. One day as he was feasting and drinking with his tribe, he saw two grim-faced men approaching with a warrant that had his name on it. They had come to throw a rope around him and drag his soul away down to the Underworld. In vain Monkey protested that he had learned the way of eternal life, they only tried to tie the rope more tightly. Monkey twisted and turned in their grasp and in the end he shook himself free. Taking the needle-sized pillar from where it lay hidden behind his ear, he blew on it until it grew to the size of a cudgel and laid about him until the two men were lying helpless on the ground. Then, swinging his cudgel about his head, he charged, bellowing, into the Underworld. The guards cringed, the clerks hid and the ten judges of the courts of Hell, hearing the commotion, came out and tried to appease Monkey.

'Bring out the register of the dead,' snarled the Monkey, 'or you will taste my cudgel.'

Fumbling, they brought out the registers and found the file containing the names of monkeys. Monkey saw his own name, and 'Soul no. 1735, Sun the Enlightened One: 342 years, a peaceful death.'

'I don't care about the years, I don't belong to this register,' he cried and, seizing a writing brush he obliterated the entry with one broad stroke, at the same time crossing out the names of all the other monkeys. He threw down the file saying 'Now you'll have no more power over me,' and thrashed his way out of Hell again. As he made his way back home he seemed to trip over a knot of grass, and woke up with a start.

'Our King is having a long snooze,' the other monkeys were saying. But Monkey knew it was no dream and was happy that he had erased his name and that of his tribe of monkeys from the register of the dead, and that King Yama had no more power over them.

Meanwhile up in Heaven the most powerful Taoist god, the Jade Emperor, was receiving complaints from all sources about Monkey's behaviour. The Dragon King of the Eastern Sea said he had stolen the iron pillar of Yü; the King of Hell complained that he had interfered in his jurisdiction. The Jade Emperor sighed and asked which one of the deities would be willing to deal with this troublesome Monkey. The Deity of the Golden Star (that is the planet Venus) volunteered to fetch Monkey up to Heaven, offer him a minor post in the administration and keep him under their eye.

Monkey was delighted to go and take up what he thought was high office in Heaven, and he was given the post of Marshal of the Heavenly Horses. The job suited Monkey very well and the heavenly horses were kept sleek and contented. After about two weeks his colleagues gave him a feast and whilst sitting at the table, Monkey asked them casually how much his salary was worth and to what grade his post belonged.
'Oh you won't get any pay,' they said. 'Your post is only honorary really, and it isn't high enough to belong to any grade.' Monkey was furious. He thought himself equal in standing with any deity in Heaven and felt he had been cheated into accepting a lowly post. He kicked over the table and stormed back home.

The Jade Emperor was most annoyed by Monkey's behaviour and sent guards to seize him from Curtain Cave; Monkey defeated them all. Even the God Nocha with his whirling arms was sent away with a smashed shoulder. The Jade Emperor was at a loss until the Deity of The Golden Star again suggested that Monkey might be brought back, this time with a grand title such as 'Great Sage, equal of Heaven' (a title without responsibility) and promises of a life of pleasure in Heaven.

Sure enough, Monkey was appeased. He returned to Heaven revelling in his triumph, and had a marvellous time doing nothing but eating, carousing with friends and enjoying himself. The Jade Emperor was worried in case such idleness bred mischief and he sent him to be guardian of the Garden of Immortal Peaches. This was the orchard where grew the peaches of immortality, whose trees bore fruit only once every six thousand years and whose fruit conferred immortality on anyone who ate it.

Monkey was pleased to be given the task and took it quite seriously. It happened that the fruits were just coming into ripeness and Monkey, knowing very well that he was not allowed to eat any, still longed to taste the beautiful, ripe, luscious fruit. In the end he sent the gardeners out of the orchard, took off his clothes and climbed a tree. Hidden among the leaves, he ate a few peaches and found them so delicious that he returned again and again.

Meanwhile the Queen Mother of the West was preparing a feast of peaches so that the immortals could renew their immortality and she sent her waiting maids to the orchard to pick the fruit. When the maids arrived they were surprised to find very few ripe fruits. One of the maids finally spotted a pink peach on a tree and she pulled down the branch to pick it, not knowing that Monkey was asleep there. The motion of the branch woke him up and he was extremely cross at being disturbed and at being caught taking a nap. The maids begged pardon on their knees, saying that they were merely preparing a banquet for the Queen Mother of the West. Monkey preened himself at the idea of a banquet and asked if he was invited, but when the maids said his name was not on the list, he again became very angry. He instantly put the maids under a fixing spell so that they could not move and went off to find out more about the feast.

Everywhere he found preparations for a great celebration. Wine was being made from the juice of jade and jasper and it smelt so good that Monkey put a sleeping spell on the attendants and drank off the best part of the supply. He ate a great many of the dishes that were being prepared, too. Half drunk, he staggered further and found himself wandering into the palace of Laozi, the Taoist saint who had written the *Tao Te Ching*. Laozi was busy in the workshop with his attendants making the drug of immortality as his contribution to the feast. The finished drugs were placed on the ground in five gourds. Monkey arrived in the workshop after all the attendants had left, and being very inquisitive about the drug, he thought he would like to taste some. So he tipped the gourds upside down,

after all the peaches and pills that he had eaten, Monkey was now so well set on the path of immortality that the crucible did him more good than harm. The great heat gave him red eyes but did not hurt him at all; instead it toughened him and made him invulnerable. At the end of forty-nine days Monkey sprang out of the crucible and immediately began fighting again, swinging his cudgel at anyone who got in his way.

At this moment Buddha himself came to see what the commotion was all about. The Buddha laughed at Monkey's antics and, taking him in his giant hand, said, 'If you can somersault your way off my palm, you can rule over the whole universe. If not, you will have to return to earth and work hard before attaining immortality.'

Monkey thought this was an easy task for the Buddha's hand seemed no more than about a *zhang* in width. He turned a great somersault, moving seventeen thousand *li* at a turn. Then after rolling over and over countless times like a wheel, he stood up. Facing him were five red pillars. 'Well,' said Monkey to himself, 'we must have come to the end of the world. I've never seen these red pillars before.' To prove that he had been there he plucked out one of his hairs and turned it into a brush with which he wrote on one of the pillars, 'Great Sage, equal of Heaven was here!' Then he urinated under the pillar and set off home quite satisfied.

'I've been to the end of the world,' he boasted to the Buddha when he saw him again.

'What nonsense,' said the Buddha, 'you never left my palm. If you want to see your own handwriting on my finger, look there!' Monkey looked, saw the writing and realized that the five red pillars were merely the five fingers of the Buddha's open hand. Knowing that he could never defeat the Buddha he tried to run away, but the Buddha's hand had already turned and clapped over him. Buddha turned his fingers into the five elements (earth, air, fire, water and wood) and created a mountain under which Monkey was safely imprisoned. He also took a powerful spell and placed it over the crack through which Monkey tried to push his head. 'Stay there, until you have expiated your sins. Then someone will come to rescue you!' said the Buddha. And there Monkey had to stay.

emptied the pills into his hands and popped them all into his mouth, just like peanuts.

After a time the effects of the jade and jasper wine began to wear off and Monkey, realizing his wickedness and the chaos he had caused, fled from Heaven and home to Curtain Cave. The mustered hosts of Heaven pursued him and there was a great battle but still none of the gods could overcome Monkey. One of the deities who came to call on the Jade Emperor to enquire about the forthcoming feast was Bodhissatva Guanyin, the Goddess of Mercy. The Jade Emperor told her about the havoc Monkey had caused and she suggested that the Jade Emperor's nephew Erlang be summoned. He was the only god strong enough to overcome Monkey and after a long struggle he managed to tie him up and bring him, bound hand and foot, to Heaven.

Laozi suggested that they should kill Monkey by burning him up in the crucible in which he made his drugs. The gods shut him firmly in, but

Tripitaka

One day, many years after Buddha had trapped Monkey in his rocky prison, Buddha was in council explaining the scriptures to the assembled immortals. 'Amongst the people in the four corners of the earth, there are some good men and some bad,' he sighed. 'I have here three volumes of the scriptures which would greatly help to convert the bad people but the books are kept in the Western Lands and I must find someone from the east who is willing to go there and take them back with him so that the people of China may learn the ways of righteousness. First, someone must be found to undertake this pilgrimage.'
'I will go and find such a pilgrim,' said the Goddess of Mercy, Guanyin, who was always conscious of the needs of the people. The Buddha was pleased and asked the Goddess to give the pilgrims as much help as possible and to keep them safe from the brigands and demons that lay along the road between China and the Western Lands.

Guanyin set off for China with one of her retainers. Sometimes she was visible, sometimes not, sometimes she was herself, sometimes disguised as a priest. Finally they arrived in Chang'an, the capital of China.

At that time the ruler of China was the Great Emperor Taizong of the Tang dynasty. The land was peaceful and Chang'an was flourishing, a bustling centre of commerce and learning. Talented men from the city were sent out to govern in every part of the country. Some twenty or so years earlier a person called Chen had been sent off to govern a district in the south. He and his wife met some robbers who killed him and carried off his wife. She, poor woman, would rather have rather died than go with them but she was expecting a child and she agreed in order to save its life. When her son was born she was determined he should not grow up among robbers so she wrapped him up warmly and tied him to a plank floating in the river. Praying that the gods would save him, she pushed the plank out into the current. The plank came to rest near a monastery where the abbot, hearing a child's cry, came out to investigate. He took the child and

brought him up as a priest and later gave him the name of Shuanzhuang. When Shuanzhuang grew up he found his mother by tracing the clothes in which he had been wrapped as a baby. Through her he learned the fate of his father, and reported it to the Emperor who had the murderers executed. Shuanzhuang later became a famous priest, revered for his character and his learning.

Meanwhile the Goddess Guanyin had shown herself to the Emperor in Chang'an and instructed him to find a priest who would go to the Western Lands to fetch the three scriptures. Shuanzhuang volunteered and the Emperor gladly accepted. He also honoured Shuanzhuang with the name of Tripitaka, this being the name of the scriptures that he was commissioned to fetch. He gave him travel papers signed and sealed by his own hand, provided him with two servants, some money and supplies and a horse, and sent him on his way.

Tripitaka had hardly left the Chinese border before the party was attacked by the demon spirits of wild animals. The two servants were killed but Tripitaka himself escaped through the help of the Deity of the Golden Star. Riding away as fast as possible he met a huntsman who gave him shelter for the night. The next morning Tripitaka was saying goodbye to the huntsman very reluctantly when suddenly they heard a loud voice like thunder echoing through the hills. 'My master has come, my master has come,' boomed the voice. As they both stood still to listen, the huntsman suddenly remembered, 'It is that ancient monkey imprisoned in the mountain. He has been there for hundreds of years. I have never heard him make such a noise. Come, let us go to him.'

Down in the valley, sure enough, they saw the face of Monkey peeping through a crack in the mountain and stretching out an arm towards them. The huntsman removed some bushes and moss so that they could see him clearly. 'Master, master' said Monkey, 'you have come at last. I have been imprisoned here for wreaking havoc in Heaven and I've been suffering here for five hundred years. The other day the Goddess Guanyin passed by and told me that if I behaved myself and became your disciple, the Buddha would release me, and allow me to go as your servant on your pilgrimage to fetch the scriptures from the Western Lands.'

Tripitaka felt very relieved when he heard this for he did not want to travel alone, but he said, 'How can I release you, I have neither an axe nor a saw.'
'You don't need either. All you have to do is to take off the spell that holds me here. Lift the slip of paper above this crack and stand well back.'

Tripitaka looked and saw the spell, written in letters of gold. He knelt to pray, then put out his hand but he had hardly touched the paper before it floated away. They hastily retreated about five *li* but Monkey cried, 'No, further, further.' So they ran a few more *li*. Suddenly there was the loudest of cracks, as though the whole earth had split open, and Monkey bounded out, delighted to be free. He bowed low before the priest, promised to do everything he asked and together they continued the journey.

Monkey served Tripitaka well and his cudgel stood them in good stead many times. As they journeyed on they arrived at a river rushing through a ravine. Suddenly a dragon rose out of the water. Monkey barely had time to snatch his master off the saddle before the horse vanished into the dragon's fearful mouth. Tripitaka was dismayed but Monkey went to the edge of the ravine and shouted, 'You rogue of a muddy worm, give us back our horse.' The dragon, who was quietly digesting the horse at the bottom of the river, came out and roared, 'Who dares to insult me?'

Monkey and the dragon started fighting like hammer and tongs but the dragon was unable to withstand Monkey and he turned back and dived into the water again. Monkey was left furious at the loss of the horse and he sped off to find Guanyin at her home at Putuo. Guanyin smiled. 'I myself placed the dragon there to be an aid to Tripitaka, for no ordinary Chinese horse can carry him through the dangers that he will encounter.'
'What kind of a help is he?' groaned the Monkey. 'My master cannot ride a dragon.'

Guanyin sighed and went back with him to the ravine where she summoned the dragon. It came out tamely and said as it bowed low, 'I'm sorry that I have eaten your horse, but I was very

hungry, and you never said you were pilgrims to the Western Lands. I wait to serve the priest to expiate my sins for I am guilty of disobedience to my father and of setting fire to his palace.'

The Goddess stepped forward and took away the pearl from under the dragon's chin. Immediately he changed into a replica of the white horse that he had eaten.

Monkey brought the white horse to Tripitaka but he was still cross about the whole incident and he protested: 'I'm not going, I'm not going any further. I can't protect my master and I'll probably end up dead myself.'
'What's the matter now?' asked Guanyin. 'You haven't come to any harm. I give you permission to call on me whenever you are in a real crisis. Come here, I'll give you something else, too.' She plucked three willow leaves from a nearby tree and put them behind Monkey's head, where they turned into three hairs. 'If you are in real need, pluck out one of these hairs and it will help you,' she said.

Monkey was satisfied and as soon as Tripitaka was on his horse, they continued their journey.

One evening they saw at a distance a small group of houses and, hoping they might find shelter there for the night, turned towards them. On the way they met a young man hurrying along who told them that the owner of the houses was a man named Gao. Gao was in serious trouble and was looking for a priest to exorcise a demon that had taken up residence. They went with the young man and Gao told them the following story. 'I have three daughters, two of whom are already married. We were looking for a suitable husband for the youngest, someone who would be willing to come and live in our house and help us in our old age. A big man came along and at first he seemed quite acceptable and did a lot of chores for us. Then he changed and began to look more and more like a pig. Worse than that, he ate too much, he ate us out of house and home. Wherever he went whirlwinds sprang up around him, and he ended by locking up our daughter in a hut at the back of the house. We haven't even seen her for six months.'

Monkey offered his services to rid them of the demon, and they all went to the hut at the back as they knew that the demon was away on some evil

business. Monkey opened the strong lock with one blow of his cudgel and they could just make out the girl crouching in the darkness, dishevelled and filthy. She ran weeping into her father's arms. Monkey sent them all away and sat down in the girl's place, taking on her outward appearance. Not long after, the fearsome Hog demon returned to the hut carrying a huge rake and swaggering about. Monkey turned himself back into his own shape and attacked him. Although the Hog used his rake skilfully, he could not hurt Monkey.

'Don't expect to beat me,' said Monkey. 'Not for nothing was I sent to guard the holy pilgrim who travels to fetch the scriptures.'

'What?' said the Hog, throwing away his rake at once. 'Why didn't you say so earlier? Ever since the Goddess of Mercy told me about the priest I have been waiting for the chance to redeem myself by serving him. I have not always been as you see me now. I used to be the captain of the guards by the Heavenly Moat until I tried to abduct Chang'o. Then the Jade Emperor sent me down to earth in this form and I must stay here until I expiate my sin. Take me to the priest and I shall go with him to the Western Lands.'

The Hog followed Monkey to Tripitaka and promised to serve him. He also swore to be a strict vegetarian, to abstain from eating all meats, the meat of animals that walk the earth, the meat of fowls that fly in the sky, the meat of fishes that swim in the water, and from the five kinds of impure plants, such as the garlics and onions. So Tripitaka called him Hog of the Eight Abstinences and Hog joined the pilgrims. The mighty rake he carried with him was useful in many adventures—even though his gluttony was not always so well under control.

On they went until they came to a broad river of quicksand. Monkey looked across with his far-seeing eyes. 'About eight hundred *li*,' he said to his companions.

Just at that moment a hideous monster rose out of the sand. He had a head of red hair, two eyes like lamps and a string of nine skulls strung around his neck. Monkey snatched Tripitaka to safety whilst Hog battled with the monster. Three times they fought, but each time the monster evaded Hog and disappeared into the quicksand

to get his strength back for another bout. Once more Monkey rushed off to Guanyin and this time she gave him a gourd, telling him to summon the monster with it, and explain to him who they were and where they were going. As soon as Monkey had done this the monster leapt out of the water and bowed before the priest. 'My apologies to you all, I have waited a long time since the Goddess of Mercy told me to expect you. I was once a serving man in Heaven, but I broke a jade dish at the banquet of peaches, so I was sent down here as punishment. I will come with you now to be your companion, and I wish to become a priest at your hand.' So Tripitaka administered his vows and tonsured his head, giving him the name of Sandman Priest. They floated the gourd on the quicksand and used it as a raft to carry them safely to the other side. So they continued on their journey to the Western Lands.

The three demons

The pilgrims met with dangers all along the way but though they suffered hardships and had to struggle and fight, the deities watched over them so that they came to no serious harm. On one occasion they were passing through a thick wood in the mountains when they saw an old man. His white hair and beard floated around his face and he leaned upon a staff, holding a string of prayer beads in his hand. 'Take care,' he cried to them. 'Watch every step you make in this wood for here lives a band of demon monsters who have fed on the flesh of men.' Having given this warning the old man disappeared.

Tripitaka was very alarmed and slid off his horse at once. Monkey, however, soared up into the clouds to pursue the old man, who was in fact none other than the Deity of the Golden Star. He was surprised to be recognized but told Monkey that there were three monsters in the wood who could hurt them. 'But should you be in real need of help, Buddha will send his army,' he added.

Monkey returned to his master and, having made sure that he was safe, went ahead to spy out the land. It was not long before he came across a demon sentry who was going round like a town crier, telling all the demons that there were strangers passing through the wood.

'Take great care of the stranger, Monkey, for he can change into any shape, even into a fly,' he warned. Monkey had in fact been buzzing around in the shape of a bluebottle so he was disconcerted and immediately changed his shape into that of a demon sentry. He soon discovered that the head demons' main target was his master, Tripitaka. 'The great roc demon has been with my other two masters and has told them that we should catch the monk from China and stew him,' said the sentry. 'Not only will his flesh be very tasty, but he is so holy that one mouthful of his flesh will confer immortality upon the eater. But who are you? I have never seen you before.'

Monkey tried to convince him that he was just another sentry demon from a different department, but the demon was suspicious and soon Monkey became so angry with him that he killed him with a blow of his fist. Then, taking on the exact appearance of the dead sentry, he followed the path and found himself outside a huge cave guarded by a crowd of lesser demons. He got past them with no difficulty and walked down a passage littered with human bones into the presence of the demon monsters. Unfortunately his disguise did not deceive them and they seized him and put him into a magic bottle.

This magic bottle was used by the monsters to destroy their most hated enemies. Once the prisoner was corked up inside it, he could never escape for the bottle was elastic and though it could be stretched to any shape, it could not be broken. As soon as Monkey was trapped inside, the magic set to work. First a magic fire engulfed him, then hundreds of poisonous snakes appeared and bit him and finally three magic fire dragons came to melt him to nothing.

Monkey, who had survived the crucible of Laozi, was not worried by the fire and when the snakes came he simply tied them together, head to tail so that they were quite harmless. The dragons, however, were more than he could manage. He felt his body begin to soften in the heat and was beginning to give up hope when he remembered the three magic hairs that the Bodhisattva Guanyin had given him long ago at the beginning of the pilgrimage. With his last strength, he felt for the hairs and found them standing up behind his head, quite untouched by the dragons' fire. He plucked one out with a prayer and immediately it turned into a magic awl. With this he quickly drilled his way out of the bottle and escaped into the cool air.

Although he was out of the bottle, he was still in the demons' wood and before long he was caught again. This time one of the demon monsters swallowed him up. Inside the monster's stomach, Monkey was quite unharmed and he proceeded to create havoc there: he pushed and he thumped and he twisted the monster's insides into knots. The monster rolled on the ground in agony. 'If you come out I'll give you anything you want,' he shouted in pain. But the other two demon monsters whispered, 'Snap his head off as he comes up.'

Fortunately Monkey heard the whisper and instead of coming up himself he poked his staff through the monster's mouth. The monster bit it so hard that he nearly broke all his teeth while Monkey twisted and turned inside again until he begged for mercy.

Monkey finally emerged when the monsters promised a safe conduct out of the wood for himself and his companions—but they had no intention of keeping their word. Within minutes they had jumped on Tripitaka, bound him and his companions and dragged them away. Monkey managed to escape by whirling his stick, and, following at a safe distance, he saw them put Tripitaka into a great steamer. A troop of lesser demons were set to fan the fire under the steamer while the three monsters retired to await the feast. Monkey crept up to the fire, blew a sleeping spell over the demons and rescued his master. Before they could escape, however, the monsters sensed that something was wrong and charged down on them, capturing Tripitaka once more.

This time Monkey was really in despair and, remembering what the Deity of the Golden Star had told him, he soared into the clouds and went to beg Buddha for help. Buddha listened patiently and then said: 'Yes, perhaps it is time that those demon monsters were put under control. One of them is the spirit of a black lion, the other of a white elephant. The spirit of the roc is the most powerful and the most ancient. He has lived almost since the creation of the world. Do not worry, Monkey, I will send two of the deities with you to deal with them.'

Monkey flew through the air ahead of the deities and battered on the door of the monsters' cave, challenging them to fight. They rushed out with their weapons but a word from the deities brought them to a halt. One of the deities seized the great roc demon and they were all carried off together to face their punishment.

Monkey found his friends trussed up in the cave like chickens and, releasing them quickly, continued with them on their journey to the west.

The arrival

They journeyed onwards for fourteen years and passed through eighty dangerous adventures. At last they came in sight of the Western Lands. The Western Lands were completely different from anywhere else they had ever seen; they were carpeted with flowers and green grass and all the people who lived there obeyed Buddha's laws. They were welcomed by a deity who directed them to the Mountain of the Soul where Buddha himself lived and where he kept the scriptures. They could already see the Mountain shining in the distance when they came to a broad river spanned by a single narrow plank. Monkey crossed and re-crossed the river on the plank without a thought of danger but Tripitaka was too frightened, for he could not swim. Then a boat arrived, rowed by a welcoming deity. 'Come, get in my boat,' he told them. 'Although it has no bottom in the middle it is safe; no waves can ever upset it and I have ferried many across these waters.' As Tripitaka hesitated, Monkey gave him a push and he slipped and fell through the bottomless middle of the boat into the river. Fortunately the deity seized him and sat him on the side where he crouched miserable and cold. As they moved away Tripitaka was horrified to see a corpse floating in the water. Monkey smiled and said, 'Don't be frightened, Master, that is your body in the water.' Hog and Sandman clapped their hands saying, 'That was you,' and

the deity said, 'That was you, congratulations.' Then Tripitaka realized that he had left his earthly body behind him and that his journey was nearly complete.

From the river they made rapid progress to the Mountain of the Soul, where they were ushered into the presence of Buddha. They prostrated themselves before him and after Buddha had given them his blessing, he sent them with two acolytes down to the stores to fetch the scriptures. There the two acolytes asked them what they had brought to pay for the scriptures. Of course they had come with nothing, and Monkey was very angry for he suspected they were being asked for a bribe. Nevertheless they were given the rolls of the scriptures (called sutras) and started out on the long journey to the east.

Before they had gone far a sudden wind rose up, snatched the rolls out of their hands and scattered them around on the ground. As they hurried to gather them up Monkey noticed that the rolls were in fact all quite blank, with no writing on them at all.
'This is no good, Master,' he said. 'We'll have to go back to Buddha and get him to put it right.' So back they went, to the amusement of the gatekeepers. Monkey bounded up to Buddha full of indignation. Buddha smiled and silenced him saying, 'The scriptures cannot be given without

any payment. You must be prepared to pay for something so valuable that it will save your soul—or your descendants will be the poorer. Because you have no money you were given blank scrolls, the wordless sutra. Though you do not know it, the wordless sutra has as much power as the ones with words. However, I suppose you people out in the east are not really clever enough to understand that. Fortunately you weren't allowed to get far with something you cannot use and now I will let you have the ones you need.'

This time Tripitaka offered his begging bowl, which was accepted. Monkey checked all the sutras to make sure that they really were the right ones and they prepared to set off once more. This time the Goddess of Mercy put in a good word for them, and instead of plodding their way overland they returned in comfort by air, on a cloud borne up by one of the Golden Guardian deities.

Meanwhile the Buddha was surveying Tripitaka's pilgrimage and the eighty dangers he had overcome. Buddha said, 'Our holiest number is nine times nine; one more is needed to make the full number up. Tripitaka must suffer one more mishap.' And he sent a message to the Golden Guardian who instantly dropped them from their comfortable cloud.

To their surprise they all landed on the ground with a bump. Tripitaka was disappointed, while Sandman said, 'Perhaps we're being offered a rest.' Monkey looked around and said, 'We've been here before. This is the river we crossed on the back of the White Turtle, and here he is.' He shouted as a white headed Turtle came out of the water and the Turtle offered to take them across the river again as he had done when they passed that way on their outward journey.
'Steady on, Turtle, you've got a precious load,' said the Monkey, and they crossed as smoothly as though they were on dry land. Half way across the river the Turtle turned to ask, 'Did you remember to find out from the Buddha what is the span of my life as a Turtle?' Tripitaka had completely forgotten in all the excitement that he had been entrusted with this task and the Turtle was so annoyed that he tipped them all into the river. Fortunately Tripitaka, having lost his earthly body, was able to swim, and they struggled to land with all the sutras—though they

had to fish some out of the water. They dried out the sutras with the help of the local people, who were delighted to see them again. The next day, as they prepared to walk back home to China, a cloud swept them up again and carried them swiftly through the air.

All this time the priests in the temples of Chang'an were praying every day for their safe return. One day they noticed that although there was no wind, the tips of the trees were all pointing to the west. One elderly priest read the sign and made ready to welcome the pilgrims home. At a great ceremony they were received by the Emperor who gave them his personal thanks.

After the sutras had been solemnly enshrined, the Golden Guardian snatched the pilgrims away again and took them back to the Mountain of the Soul to the presence of Buddha.
'Your pilgrimage is now complete,' said Buddha, 'Your goal is achieved and your disciples have expiated the sins that they had committed. You, Tripitaka, will remain here by my side as a deity. Though you do not know it, you were once my disciple here but you were proud and would not listen to reason. To punish you, you were sent to earth to undertake this pilgrimage. Now you may return to your rightful place.

'You, Sun the Enlightened One, are also forgiven. For your good deeds and your devotion to your master, I now make you a deity, the Victorious One in Battle.

'I make you, Hog of the Eight Abstinences, an acolyte, Altar Cleaner-in-Chief.' At this Hog protested loudly, 'They have all become deities,' he said, 'why not me.'

The Buddha said, 'Because your appearance is too ungainly; besides you eat too much. If you can clear all the altars in my temples of their offerings, you can eat to your heart's content.

'Sandman, for your reward I raise you to the rank of an Arhat, a companion of Buddha.

'Horse, you may return to your father in the Western Ocean. He has forgiven your disobedience.'

The horse swiftly resumed his own shape and swam away. The others took their place in the ranks of the deities, the arhats and the acolytes. The sound of the recitation of the sutras filled Heaven once more.

Tales of faith and loyalty

During the third century BC the First Emperor of Chin ruled over the whole of China. His vast empire was made up of many conquered states but although he had defeated so many smaller forces he was still very afraid of the barbarian tribes. These were nomads, mighty warriors who roamed the steppes to the north and west of China on horseback and the Emperor feared that one day they would sweep down and overwhelm his empire. In order to defend the country he began building the Great Wall of China.

The Great Wall was to be a tall, impregnable line of defence, strong enough to withstand any attack. Built of great slabs of stone hewn from solid rock, it was over forty feet tall and in places the top was broad enough for eight men to march abreast. At intervals there were guard towers on the top of which beacon fires were lit to warn if the tribesmen were gathering to attack.

The Wall's path lay along the north-western frontier of China and passed through some of its most inhospitable country—high mountains, deserts and scrub. Because it was so far north, the winters were long and bitter and food and shelter were hard to find. The first Emperor was a cruel tyrant and used forced labour to build the Wall. The men he commanded to work there were not criminals or slaves, but honest citizens and because of the hardships of the terrain and the difficulty of the work, many never returned home again. People dreaded the summons that sent them to exile and almost certain death and a folksong of the time asked: 'Have you seen the foot of the Wall, the skeletons of men leaning one upon the other?'

The diviners said that ten thousand men would have to die before the Wall could be completed but still the work went on; new workers were continually rounded up and building material was diverted to the great project. The people became desperate. Then, somewhere a whisper started that if a man called Wan (whose name in Chinese mean 'ten thousand') were killed at the Wall, then his death would be worth the death of ten thousand innocent men and the Wall could be finished without the loss of any more lives. Just as the rumour was gathering strength a young man with the surname of Wan was recruited in the city of Suzhou and when the officers saw his name at the head of their list, they took it as a sign that this was the man the prophecy referred to.

The unfortunate recruit was Wan Shiliang, a young man from a good family in Suzhou. He was naturally very frightened when he heard the prophecy and ran away from home in the hope of avoiding capture. For several miserable days he travelled southwards, trying to get as far as he could in the opposite direction to the Great Wall but having no real idea how he could hide from the Emperor's officers.

One day as he was walking along the road he saw a cavalcade of horsemen approaching. In the distance he thought he could make out the pennants of the official recruiting officers and he was so alarmed that the Emperor might have caught up with him that he ran off the road and leaped over the first wall he saw. Not daring to move, he crouched close to the ground and waited, holding his breath. After allowing enough time for the horsemen to pass by, he picked himself up and looked around to see where he was.

Wan found himself in a rich man's garden, surrounded by the high wall he had jumped in his rush for safety. The garden was secluded and calm with trees planted around a lake beside an ornamental pavilion, a kind of decorated summer house. As it was high summer, the leaves were lush and green and the noise of birds and insects filled the air. As he looked around, peering through the trees, Wan saw a young lady come into the garden. She was beautiful and richly dressed and she came skipping over the grass without a care in the world, chasing the brightly coloured butterflies as they darted to and fro over the flowers. As Wan watched in admiration, she ran along the bank of the lake and, not looking where she was going, slipped off and fell into the water. Wan bounded from his hiding place and waded into the lake, catching hold of her as she struggled, screaming in the water.

The girl's cries brought people running into the garden and her parents were horrified to see an unknown young man, dusty and dirty, pulling at their daughter who seemed to be half drowning in the lake. At first they assumed that Wan had attacked the girl but when she had been rescued and was calm enough to talk sensibly, they realized that, far from pushing her into the water Wan was responsible for saving her life.

The parents now faced another problem for in old China etiquette forbade young men and women who were not related even to see, let alone touch each other. Yet here was this stranger carrying the girl out of the lake in his arms and now staring at her as if he could not take his eyes off her for a minute. Seeing that the girl, too, appeared to be in love, and having discovered that Wan came from a good family, they decided to allow the young people to get married. So Wan married the girl, whose name was Meng Jiangnü and, hardly believing his good fortune, settled down happily with his wife in his father-in-law's house.

However, this unusual way of acquiring a son-in-law soon spread to other ears and before long the local magistrate heard about it. Officers were sent to the Meng household and Wan was dragged off to fulfill the cruel prophecy at the Great Wall, leaving his young wife behind.

As the summer passed and the first winds of autumn began to blow, Meng Jiangnü thought constantly of her husband. She hoped that somehow his life might have been spared—and then immediately began to worry about the bitter cold of winter at the northern frontier. She made up her mind to make him a suit of warm clothes and to take it to him herself at the Great Wall. Having stitched the clothes with loving care she managed to persuade her reluctant parents to allow her to make the journey and, with a small bundle of her own, and a larger one of her husband's winter clothes, she took an umbrella and set out.

It was several thousand miles from her home to the Great Wall and she had to pass through very difficult country and risk many dangers on the way. A young, beautiful girl like Meng Jiangnü would not normally have needed to step out of her own front door even to buy needle and thread—all her wants would be attended to by a host of maids and menservants. Now she was braving all kinds of hardships in order to be with her husband—without even knowing that he was still alive. Some versions of the story tell how her devotion was rewarded by many supernatural beings who helped her on her way. One legend tells how when she came to cross the broad Yangtze River, there were no boats in sight and no way of reaching the other side. Meng Jiangnü wept and sadly dabbled her fingers in the water, gently patting the water surface. To her surprise, when she did this the level of the river sank a little; she patted it again and it sank again until finally she was able to clear a path through the river and walk across on dry land. When she came to the Yellow River she again could see no way of crossing and she threw her skirt over her eyes and waded into the water, preferring to drown rather than give up her journey and return home. As she waded in a gentle wind picked her up and when she opened her eyes again she was several miles away, on the further side of the river.

Nearing the end of her journey at last, she reached the bleak north where the Wall was being built. The sun was setting and she did not know in which direction to go. As she stood still looking around her, a flock of ravens swooped over her, cawing raucously, and settled on a tree nearby. She turned to watch them and two birds left the flock and flew around her, seeming to ask her to follow them, then took off in a definite direction. She took this as a sign and followed them until she came to a small village where a kindly old couple gave her shelter.

The old couple knew about the prophecy and it turned out that Wan had been taken through the village not very long ago and that they had seen him. They had heard he had reached the Wall at a point not far from the village and the very next day Meng Jiangnü gathered up her bundles and made her way to the spot.

At the Wall, workers were hurrying to and fro and at first she could find no-one to ask. Then she came to the foreman in charge of the building work, and, fearing the worst, asked him if he knew her husband.

'You have come too late', replied the foreman. 'I remember him well—he came to fulfill some prophecy. Of course we set him to work immediately but he did not last long, he was not strong enough and he died in a matter of weeks. We buried him along with the others in the foundation of the wall.'

The Chinese used to believe that the souls of the dead would never find eternal rest unless their bodies had been given proper burial, so Meng Jiangnü asked tearfully where her husband had been buried so that she could gather his bones and take them home for the right ceremonies to be performed. The foreman led her to a part of the Wall.

'This is where we put him,' he said, 'but the Wall has been built over thirty feet above him now. You have no hope of collecting his bones. Besides, how will you distinguish his among so many?'

Meng Jiangnü sank to her knees and began to weep. She wept for all the love she bore her husband, for the pain and suffering he must have undergone—and for the hardships of her own journey. So intense and powerful were her tears that the full height of the Wall where her husband lay split in half from the top to the foundations. As the stones came tumbling down the earth opened to reveal the bones of all the men who had died with her husband at the Wall.

As the foreman had guessed, she had no way of knowing which bones had been her husband's but she prayed to the gods for guidance and once again they helped her. As she wept she bit her little finger until the blood ran.

'Let my blood fall on these unfortunate bones,' said Meng Jiangnü,' and when it falls on those of my husband, let it sink into them and be absorbed, for we are one flesh and one blood.'

The blood she sprinkled over the heap of bones dripped off all but one skeleton and every spot that fell on those bones sank and disappeared. She knew then that these were her husband's remains.

News of the miracle spread like wildfire and before Meng Jiangnü had left the village the Emperor of Chin, who was there inspecting the building, heard the story. Angrily he sent for her. 'Who are you?' he thundered. 'Who dares to disturb the imperial work with weeping?'

Meng Jiangnü was not at all frightened. 'My husband was put to death here by your cruelty,' she replied. 'May you who rob others of their lives never enjoy life yourself.'

The Emperor was about to order her instant death when he looked again and noticed how young and beautiful she was. The sight of her beauty softened his heart and he began to have other ideas about her. 'You are a brave young woman,' he said in a kindly way. 'This is no place for you. Come to my palace and I will give you everything you desire—riches, fine clothes and jewelry, more than you ever imagined possible—if you will be my wife.'

Meng Jiangnü was about to give him an angry refusal when she realized she could make use of his infatuation. 'I will agree on three conditions,' she said.

'Only three?' asked the Emperor, 'I will accept thirty. You have only to name them.'

'Firstly, you must build a tall bridge spanning the great river beyond the Wall.'

'It is done,' said the Emperor.

'Secondly, you must raise on the bank of the river a magnificent tomb for my husband, built exactly to my specifications.'

'At once,' said the Emperor.

'Thirdly, you must wear mourning and be the chief mourner at the burial, offering the best offerings to my husband as if you were honouring your very own father.'

The Emperor was reluctant to agree to the third condition but in the end he accepted.

The bridge and the tomb were soon completed and the funeral ceremony was performed. Meng Jiangnü and the Emperor, dressed in the deepest mourning, shared in an elaborate ritual for the dead soul of Wan. When it was all over, the Emperor turned to Meng Jiangnü and said: 'Come now, take off your mourning clothes and put on the bright silk garments I have prepared so that we can have our marriage feast.'

Meng Jiangnü broke away and ran to the bridge that the Emperor had built for her. Standing on its highest point she cried defiantly 'Do you imagine that I would stain the memory of my husband by giving myself to you for money and jewels? You will always be hated for your tyranny. The Wall you have built will be useless against the barbarians and will protect neither you nor your empire from defeat and death.'

With these words she jumped from the parapet into the middle of the river and was drowned.

The Great Wall of China never did keep out the barbarians, impressive though it was to look at. Time and again the barbarian hordes raided across the border and eventually they conquered China altogether. The Empire founded by the first Emperor of Chin lasted no longer than his own tyrannous reign.

Dong Yong, the faithful son

There was once a couple who had their only child when they were both growing old in years. The son, whose name was Dong Yong, was a clever child and was always very loving towards his elderly parents. Before long his father died and the widowed mother supported her son by her sewing, working hard to send him to school and keeping nothing for herself. Her great ambition was that he should become a scholar and enter for the civil service examinations, which were held throughout the country to select the cleverest young men to serve the Emperor. After a few years Dong Yong was old enough to enter for the preliminary examinations which were held in each province of the Empire. They waited anxiously for the results and when they came at last, Dong Yong's name was at the top of the list. Mother and son were both very happy but the strain of seeing her son through the examinations proved too much for the mother and she no sooner heard of his success than she collapsed and died.

Dong Yong was now in great difficulties. The money that his father had left had all been spent long ago and he had no-one to support him. It seemed certain that he would have to forget his ambitions to serve the Emperor and try to make a living in a more humble way. However, his greatest worry was how to provide his mother with a decent burial; without the correct ceremonies and proper period of mourning, he knew that her soul would not find rest. After a great deal of thought he decided that the only way to raise money was to sell himself into slavery.

Dong found a man named Fu who was willing to buy him and who agreed to wait until after the burial before receiving him into his household. With the money he was given, Dong was able to make all the necessary arrangements for the funeral and on the appointed day he followed his mother's body to the grave. Overwhelmed with grief beside the grave, he fainted right away. When he came round he saw a young and beautiful woman standing beside him. 'Who are you that has come to mourn my mother?' asked Dong.

'I am your wife,' she replied. 'My name is Dagu and before your mother died she promised my family that we would marry. Now we must carry out her wishes and be married immediately.'

Dong Yong was astonished as he had never heard of any marriage plans but he said: 'We need witnesses to a marriage.'

Dagu pointed at the trees around them. 'These shall be our witnesses,' she said.
'Yes, if they agree,' said Dong Yong.

Dagu waved her hands at the trees and with a sighing voice they all replied 'Yes.'

The marriage was now complete and Dagu went with Dong Yong to the family who owned him. They were surprised to see him with a wife but she explained that she had come to help him earn his freedom and that she was an expert spinner and weaver. 'That remains to be seen,' said Fu sceptically and he asked Dagu to make and embroider a pair of slippers for his wife as a test. Within a day Dagu brought to him the most beautiful pair of silk slippers he had ever seen: the flowers and birds that formed the intricate pattern were so real they almost seemed alive. Next he set her to work on the loom and within a few days she had produced the most beautiful piece of silk brocade, woven in all the colours of the rainbow. Fu and his wife were delighted with the work but they realized that no mortal hand could have made such marvellous things and, fearing to offend the spirits, they released Dong Yong from slavery and forgave him his debt.

After Dong Yong and Dagu were freed, Dagu worked at her sewing and weaving and supported her husband until he had finished his studies and was able to travel to the capital to take the final examinations. Again he passed top of the list and was given an important post at court. Dagu gave birth to their son soon afterwards and everything seemed set for a happy and prosperous life. One day, soon after Dong Yong had been given an audience by the Emperor and taken up his new appointment, Dagu came to him. 'Now that you are well started in life,' she told him, 'I can tell you the truth. You must have wondered how I came to be standing next to you at your mother's grave and I am sure you have often wanted to ask me the real story of our marriage contract.'
'That is true,' replied Dong Yong. 'At first I was

certainly puzzled that my mother had never discussed you with me. But after we were married I really never thought about it again. If you wish to tell me something now, however, please continue. Nothing you can say will anger me.'
'The truth is that I am not an ordinary human woman,' she said, 'but one of the heavenly maids. We saw your devotion to your mother from up there and I was chosen to come down to earth to help you. Now that you are successful and have no need of my support, I must return to heaven.'
'How can you leave me now?' cried Dong Yong. 'And how can you leave our son?' But his pleading was in vain. Dagu insisted that her place was in heaven and, putting their small son in his arms, she left the house, never to be seen again.

Though Dong Yong never saw his wife again, it seems likely that, from heaven, she continued to watch the family's progress for Dong Yong became a very high official at court and his son was equally successful when he grew up.

The Swordmaker's son

In all ancient cultures objects made from metals, and the smiths who produced them, were greatly valued. China was no exception. Metal weapons, especially swords, were referred to as 'precious' and were treated almost as if they had magical powers. Weapon makers, though seldom rich or powerful, were always respected people.

Once in the Kingdom of Chu there lived a very famous swordmaker called Ganjiang. His wife, also a skilled smith, was called Moye. One day the King of Chu summoned Ganjiang and ordered him to make him two swords. 'Let them be the best swords that you have ever forged in your life,' he commanded, glaring fiercely at Ganjiang, 'or else you will have cause to regret it.'

Ganjiang and Moye took the greatest care over the forging of these swords. Every process of every stage was done twice over so that the swords that finally emerged would be twice as strong as any others. It soon began to be whispered that the care and skill being lavished on the king's new swords were making them into something very special indeed.

Ganjiang and Moye worked night and day, stopping only for food and brief snatches of sleep. Even so, it was three years before they had made the swords to their satisfaction, tempered and tested them and tempered them again, polished and sharpened them until the long blades glinted and gleamed. The two swords were a matching pair, almost exactly the same except that one was more slender than the other. They were made so that they fitted together and could both be sheathed in the same scabbard. The blades were long, the handles well balanced and beautifully carved. The blades flashed with a cold light like the reflection of the moon on autumn water; a hair floating down against the edge was instantly severed; cutting into iron or into another weapon was like slicing through mud. No-one had ever seen anything to compare with these weapons either for beauty or deadly efficiency and in honour of their makers they called the slenderer sword, the female, Moye and the wider one, the male, Ganjiang.

When the king heard that the swords were complete he was both happy and anxious—pleased that with such swords he could conquer the world but worried that once everyone knew the quality of the weapons, others might commission similar ones for themselves from Moye and Ganjiang and threaten him once again. To avoid this risk, the king decided that he would have to find an excuse to have the swordmaker killed.

Ganjiang was well aware of the danger he faced. From the frequent messages that had passed between the palace and the forge during the three years the swords had been making, he had guessed that the king both wanted to possess the swords and hated and feared their maker. Moye was pregnant when the swords were ready and Ganjiang laid careful plans.

'The king is a suspicious and ruthless man,' he told her as he prepared to set out for the palace. 'He distrusts my skill as a swordmaker and I fear the worst. I am going to see him now but to test his good faith I shall only give him the female sword. I have already hidden the male sword. If I should be killed and the child you bear is a boy, tell him this when he grows to be a man. "As you walk out of the gate and look towards the southern mountain, a pine grows upon a stone and the sword is in the tree." If he can find the sword then he will avenge my death.'

Ganjiang made Moye repeat the message several times until he was satisfied she knew it by heart. Then, looking around at his house and forge for what he feared was the last time, he set out for the palace.

When he arrived at court he ceremoniously handed the female sword to the King.
'What's this?' cried the King, angrily.
'This is my finest sword,' answered Ganjiang politely, 'forged in my own fire with all the skill my art can bring.'
'I ordered you to make two swords,' stormed the King. 'I wait for three years while you take your time to make them and now what do I find: you bring only one. What have you to say for yourself? This is contempt for my royal command.'
'The making of a sword such as this is no easy matter,' answered Ganjiang. 'If you will give me a few more weeks. . . .'

'Silence,' commanded the King. 'Take him away.' And before Ganjiang could protest, the soldiers seized him and led him to his death.

After Ganjiang's death, his wife Moye gave birth to a boy, whom she brought up with the greatest care. He grew up to be a fine, well-built boy. The only thing that was odd about his appearance was that his eyebrows were set wide apart so that people used to tease him, saying that he had the width of a whole foot between his brows. The boy often asked his mother what had happened to his father but she usually managed to put him off and change the subject. At first it was too painful for her to speak of the husband she had lost and, fearing that she would lose her son, too, when he knew the truth, she delayed telling him from year to year. When she judged he was old enough to fight she told him the whole story.

The boy was as angry as she had expected and immediately vowed to avenge his father.
'But what happened to the other sword?' he asked. 'I shall need the best weapon in the world if I am to fight this evil king.'

Moye remembered Ganjiang's final instructions. 'As you walk out of the gate and look towards the southern mountain, a pine grows upon a stone and the sword is in the tree,' she said. 'Those were you father's last words to me and, if you can interpret them correctly, they will lead you to the hidden sword.'

The boy puzzled over the words for a long time without being able to make any sense of them. There was no mountain to the south of the house and no pine growing nearby. Then, early one morning, as he stood in the front doorway looking towards the south he noticed something for the first time. The roofed gateway to the courtyard in front of the house was raised on a slab of stone and the roof itself was supported by pine pillars with stone bases.
'I wonder,' he said to himself, 'Could these pillars be the "pine growing upon a stone"?' And taking an axe he struck the pillar nearest the house and split it open. There, hidden in a neatly carved hollow, he found the gleaming sword, its long blade shining as brightly as ever in the morning sun. Pausing only to test its weight and to say goodbye to his mother, he set off to avenge his father.

That night the King of Chu had a frightening dream. A young man approached him with a bright sword in his hand.
'I have come to avenge my father's death,' he said.

The king woke in terror and immediately summoned his court to ask for their advice. 'What did the young man look like?' asked the counsellors. The king described Ganjiang's tall, handsome son carefully. 'But the most remarkable thing about him was his eyebrows,' he said. 'They were set so far apart. With those brows, his face is quite unmistakeable.'

Pictures were painted from the king's description and posters were nailed up all over the town offering rewards for the capture of a dangerous killer. When Ganjiang's son arrived at the city he found his own face staring at him from every side and fled in terror to the mountains.

The boy hid in the mountains for several days trying to work out what to do now that his plan had obviously been anticipated. One dawn as he sat weeping after a long, sleepless night, a traveller dressed in black approached him.
'What is the matter, young man?' asked the stranger. Something about him made the young man confide in him and when he had told his story, the stranger spoke solemnly. 'The King of Chu is an evil tyrant indeed. It is impossible to count the number of people he has murdered and the people who manage to live under his cruel rule do so in perpetual fear. I am a warrior without a country—for my country has been conquered by him like so many others. If I avenge your wrong I shall be avenging my country, too, and all the suffering people he rules.'
'Will you help me, then?' asked the boy.
'Yes, I will help you, but I shall need your help, too. Are you willing to make a sacrifice?'

Eagerly the youth asked what he should do.
'If you have been into the city you will have seen the posters offering a large reward for your head,' said the stranger. 'If I were to chop off your head I could take it to the king and he, thinking I am a friend, will allow me to come near him. Then I will kill him for you.'

The boy looked hard at the stranger in black then quietly took his father's sword from the scabbard and, with a swift blow, struck off his own head. His body remained upright as he

thrust both the sword and his head into the stranger's arms.

'Do not be afraid,' said the stranger. 'I will not fail you.' Then the body collapsed to the ground.

Sighing, the stranger wiped off a slight smear of blood from the bright edge of the sword, wrapped the head carefully, sheathed the sword and buried the boy's body. Then he set off for the city. At the palace gates he boldly announced his business and was ushered at once into the king's presence. The king took one look at the severed head and, recognizing the face from his dream, he smiled gratefully at the stranger.

'First throw this villainous head to the dogs,' he commanded his servants, 'then give this stranger food and drink, for he has served me better than he knows. It is indeed the man from my dreams.'

'Wait,' said the stranger. 'If the young man appeared to you in a dream he must have spirit powers. You must destroy the head by boiling it, otherwise who knows what mischief it may do.'

The king thought this was wise advice and he gave orders for a huge cauldron to be filled with water and heated. Then he himself threw the head into it. 'So perish all my enemies,' he thundered.

For three days and nights the cauldron boiled and bubbled yet the head showed no sign of change. Instead it floated on the surface, fixing an accusing eye on anyone who passed by. Finally the stranger asked the king to inspect it, saying that the royal presence might have some effect. Reluctantly, the king agreed and followed the stranger to the place where the cauldron was standing over the fire. As he peered fearfully in, the stranger whipped out the sword which he had carried hidden in his clothes all this time and struck off the king's head so that it fell straight into the boiling water. With a triumphant laugh he then struck off his own head and this, too, fell into the cauldron, whereupon all three heads instantly distintegrated.

By the time the cauldron had been removed from the fire all three heads were quite unrecognizable so they were all buried together in a large tomb which, for many generations, continued to be called the Tomb of the Three Noblemen. Ganjiang and the stranger's country-men were all avenged and the tyrant's rule was ended.

119

Gods and superstitions

Early Chinese religious beliefs held that everything in life had its own guardian spirit and that even inanimate objects had an existence of their own. In popular supersition this belief was extended to even the most humble man-made objects: houses, stoves, cooking pots and pans all had guardians who had the power to make the objects work properly and help the people who used them to succeed in what they were doing. To keep the guardians in a good temper, people made offerings to them and even dedicated temples to the more powerful spirits. Religious cults grew up and became an accepted part of the routine of life.

Certain unpredictable forces in life such as the weather and the elements could be man's greatest enemies. They were considered to be important gods and were worshipped with full ceremony. In paintings and carvings they are shown with all the paraphernalia of their powers.

These cults were scorned as superstitions by the better educated members of society though they, too, resorted to them at times of great stress and there were few houses indeed without their statuettes of the household gods. Some of the stories that grew up around the cults were humorous in tone, an indication that the Chinese attitude towards these gods and spirits was not wholly serious.

As in all societies the cooking stove or hearth was regarded as the central point of a household and the god who presided over it was naturally an important figure. In the old days every Chinese home had a small niche in the wall above the cooking stove where an image of the god was kept, with an incense stick burning before it. Every year at the New Year the soot-blackened image was burned, for that was the time when the stove god went up to Heaven to make his report to the High God on how the family had been behaving all the year round. Having observed them from his niche in the kitchen he knew all about them and their future was fixed on the basis of his report.

The stove god was sent off on his journey to Heaven with some ceremony. People lit firecrackers and offered the god a good meal, to win his favour. Sometimes he was offered honey so that he would speak only sweet words about them, sometimes more drastic action was taken and he was given a sweetmeat so sticky and glutinous that it would stick his mouth together. The idea was that when he was asked to make his report, his lips would literally be sealed so that he would only be able to nod his head to show that the family had been good.

Some of the stories that have grown up around the stove god say that he was originally a human being. There are many versions but they all have the same basic outline. He was a good, kind man when he was alive, but very poor, so poor that in the end he could not afford to keep his wife and had to give her to someone else in marriage. Some years later he was begging his way through the town when he came to the house where his wife now lived. When he recognized her, he felt so ashamed that he tried to hide himself in the cooking stove. Unfortunately he had not realized that it was red hot and he was killed. As he had been an honest man all his life, the High God made him the god of the stove.

Door gods

The gods of the door had the important task of keeping undesirable visitors away from the house. People used to pin pictures on either side of the door, showing fierce warriors whose terrifying faces and dangerous weapons would frighten away evil spirits. Like the image of the stove god, the pictures were changed every year.

At some time in China's long history, the door gods became identified with two warriors who served the first Emperor of the Tang dynasty, in the seventh century AD.

The Emperor had fallen sick and at night in his feverish sleep he saw demons rampaging around his bed. During the daytime he was undisturbed. Everyone became very concerned about the Emperor's life and two of his best warriors offered to stand guard outside his door all night to protect him from the demons. The Emperor slept well that night for the first time since his illness and from then onwards, he continued to improve in health. At last, when he was strong and well again, he allowed the warriors to sleep at night again but he asked painters to make two pictures of them looking as fierce as they could. These he hung beside the door so that the demons would never dare to return.

The gods of the elements

The gods of the elements were among the most powerful of the guardian spirit gods and included the gods of thunder, lightning and wind. The Thunder God was an ugly creature with bat wings, clawed feet and an eagle's beak. He made his thunder by clashing a chisel and hammer on his drums. The Lightning God was female and she sent out streaks of lightning by projecting beams of light from the mirrors she held in her hands. The Wind God was an old man who carried leather bags in which he imprisoned the winds. Together they controlled the forces of the storms and, if not correctly worshipped, could cause untold damage, smashing down trees and houses, ruining crops and flooding valuable land.

Of the three, the Thunder God appears most often in myths and legends. As well as controlling the thunder, he also used his powers to punish serious wrongdoers. Sometimes, however, he was helpful to humans.

One story tells how a youth who was out cutting firewood in the high mountains took refuge from a thunderstorm under a large tree. Suddenly there was a loud clap of thunder right overhead and the tree was struck by lightning. Looking up, the youth saw an ugly creature with a blue face and bird's claws stuck in the cleft of the tree. The creature said ruefully: 'I am the Thunder God. In splitting this tree I have trapped myself completely. If you will free me I will reward you well.'

The woodcutter agreed, and freed the unfortunate god by driving wedges into the tree and enlarging the cleft in which he was stuck. The god disappeared as soon as he was free but later he gave the boy a book from which he learned how to bring thunder and rain and how to cure sickness. 'When you want rain,' said the Thunder God, 'all you have to do is call one of my brothers. Don't call on me unless it is really necessary because I do a great deal of damage.'

The woodcutter had great success with his book and became quite famous in the area. Then one day he had too much wine to drink and was arrested by the police for disorderly behaviour. As they led him into court he called on the

Thunder God to help him and the god thundered so powerfully that all the houses in the town shook and rattled on their foundations. The magistrate was very frightened and he released the woodcutter at once before the Thunder God could do any serious damage.

Another story tells how a harmless old woman had her arm broken when she was struck by lightning. She was just cursing her bad luck when a voice from above said: 'Sorry, I made a mistake.' A bottle fell out of the sky and landed on the ground in front of her as the voice went on: 'Rub the contents of this bottle on your arm and it will be healed at once.'

The old woman did as she was told and her arm was mended immediately. The bottle disappeared into space as mysteriously as it had come.

Gods of the stars

Like all peoples, the Chinese were fascinated by the stars and made up stories about them. The story of the herd boy and the weaving girl on page 41 is just one of many that give the stars human connections.

The position of stars in the sky naturally meant that they overlooked the activities of human beings and possibly also gave them powers to influence their lives. Some became worshipped as gods. The Dipper constellation (*Ursa major*) has almost the same name in Chinese, *Beidoushing*, meaning the Northern Dipper Star. Beidoushing was a goddess, known as the Mother Dipper or, in some parts of China, as the Queen of Heaven. She was a preserver of mankind and was sometimes given the same powers as the goddess of Mercy, Guanyin. She was also linked to the goddess Arichi of Indian Brahmnin mythology, who was the personification of light and Goddess of the Dawn. Beidoushing was not always a female god: sometimes it was regarded as male, the God of Long Life.

One of the stars in the constellation was worshipped as the star god Kui, who became the patron of literature and especially of examination candidates. According to one legend there was once a scholar named Kui who was unfortunate

enough to have an extremely ugly face. He achieved the highest distinction in the imperial examinations but the sight of Kui's face so appalled the emperor that he refused to give him his rightful place in the government. Kui was so disheartened that he committed suicide but a sea monster took him on his back and the gods sent him to the sky as a god.

By a twist of fate, in popular superstition Kui became the patron of examination candidates, probably because he had passed his own examinations so well—though the success did him very little good. The Kui Star has often been represented in paintings, not as a real person but as a figure made of the Chinese character *Kui*, with its strokes tilted to look liked a strange, demonic person. In one hand he holds a writing brush and with one of his feet he kicks at the Dipper Star. These pictures became a kind of good luck card to send to examination candidates before their ordeal and the expression 'kicking the dipper' came to mean passing examinations. Pictures of Kui appear on inkstones, brush holders and many other scholarly instruments. Sometimes he is shown with a carp. Carps spawn in the sea but return to the rivers to grow. The journey upstream is full of perils and the fish often have to leap upwards to reach a higher level—another metaphor for successful examination candidates.

The Star of the North Pole (also known as Taiyi) was often worshipped in the belief that he could grant people's wishes. There was once a young girl, as good as she was beautiful. Unfortunately her mother fell ill and there seemed to be no cure for her sickness. The girl had heard that if you worshipped the Pole Star sincerely every day for a hundred days he would grant any wish you asked. So every day she nursed her mother tenderly and every night she prayed to the Pole Star, lighting incense sticks and honouring him with all the correct ceremonies.

The hundred days passed at last and as she was kneeling as usual to pray, an old man with a long, white beard appeared before her and asked her to make a wish.
'I wish that my mother may be fully restored to health,' she said without hesitation. The Pole Star approved her wish and it was granted

immediately; by the next morning, the mother had recovered.

The story does not end quite there, however. As soon as news of the mother's recovery became known, families of eligible young men began to make offers of marriage for the daughter. Eventually the mother made her choice and it proved to be a very successful match. The young couple prospered and the whole family became both wealthy and happy.

In the same town there was another girl who was rich and spoilt and had everything in the world that she could wish for. She heard of the young girl's success with worshipping the Pole Star and, seeing that it had brought her a happy marriage as well as her original wish, she decided to try the same thing for herself. With unusual perseverance she managed to worship the Pole Star every night for a hundred days until at last the important night approached and the devotion was complete. Sure enough, the Pole Star appeared again.

The girl was so dumbfounded by the sight that her mind fell into a whirl of wishes—for beauty, riches, a good husband, a new dress and a hundred other things. There were so many things to ask for that she could not say a single word. The Pole Star waited patiently for her to speak but all she could do was cover her mouth in dismay with one hand and with the other point helplessly at the god. In the end the Pole Star nodded his head and disappeared.

The next day the girl found herself wth a fine growth of beard, as white as that of the Pole Star himself. Since she had been unable to speak, the Pole Star had interpreted her gestures in his own way and, thinking she was asking for a beard, had given her once just like his own.

Lord Guan

Some gods had been popular heroes when they were alive on earth. Men who had been more virtuous than others or who had been great benefactors of society were often deified after their death and temples were built in their name, much as Christians canonize saints and dedicate churches to them. One of the most popular was Lord Guan or Guang Gong, the god of the martial arts. People also called on him to protect them against demons and because he was supposed to be able to recite a difficult ancient classic story by heart, he was also a patron god of scholars.

Lord Guan's human name was Guan Yü and he lived in the second century AD. He was one of the military followers of the King of Shu, Liu Bei. The story of his life as the faithful follower of Liu Bei was told in the popular novel *The Romance of the Three Kingdoms* which told in fictional form the history of the period when three different kings fought each other for supremacy in China.

Guan Yü was at first simply a military hero, strong as a giant and invincible in battle. He was renowned for his courage and loyalty but he was also such a generous and good man that everyone loved him. After his death, in popular legend he soon became a folk hero with special powers and it was not long before he was raised from being a hero to being a god. By the seventh century, Buddhists had even made him the guardian of a monastery and the Taoists also recognized his power against all sorts of demons. Not long after, temples were built honouring him alone and in time every town had a temple dedicated to his name.

Many of Guan Yü's adventures were retold in popular novels and plays. In the plays he was always shown as a character with a face painted completely red. This is how he obtained his ruddy complexion.

As a young man, Guan Yü was intelligent and daring, always full of strength and willing to use it to help those who were weaker than himself. One day he heard that the son of the local governor, a great bully of a man, had kidnapped the daughter of an honest citizen. The poor man was powerless to do anything to protect his daughter and it looked as if the bully would be allowed to keep the girl. Then Guan Yü stepped in; he killed the bully and rescued the girl, taking her home to her father's house. Knowing that the governor would try to avenge his son's death, he took refuge in the temple. Sure enough, the governor sent his officers to capture Guan Yü and they set fire to the temple to force him out into the street again. Guan Yü remained inside until the flames were licking all around him, then burst out and, taking his pursuers by surprise, he killed them all. He ran to a stream to wash and cool his body and noticed from his reflection in the water that the fire had changed his complexion to bright red. He was therefore able to escape from the town unrecognized and went off to join the forces of Liu Bei in Shu.

While he was serving Liu Bei several of the commanders joined their armies to fight against a rebel they all hated. Seeing that he was outnumbered, the rebel halted his men and sent out his champion and challenged all the commanders to single combat. At first no-one dared to take up the challenge for the champion was known to be a fierce and treacherous fighter. Then one of them turned to Guan Yü and offered him a cup of warm wine as a sign that he should fight and win. Guan Yü took the hint, left the table where they were all eating and went out to fight the rebel champion. He had defeated him and was back in his usual place at the table before the wine had time to cool.

On another occasion he was pierced by a poisoned arrow during a battle. His left arm swelled up and the surgeons had to operate. In those days, before anaesthetics had been discovered, it required great courage to undergo an operation. Guan Yü sat down at table with one of his friends and began to play a game of chess as the surgeon prepared his instruments. The surgeon had to cut away a large part of the flesh and scrape the bone clear of poison before applying soothing herbs and binding the wound up again. All through this painful procedure, Guan Yü remained absorbed in his game and never looked up or gave any sign of feeling pain. When the arm was safely bandaged once more, Guan Yü calmly finished his game.

Guan Yü continued to serve the king for many

The God of Marriage

In old China marriages were arranged by families for their children; wise parents chose partners carefully and arranged marriages were often very happy. Naturally there was an element of chance about any marriage and they did not always succeed but people believed that marriages were in any case made in Heaven and were beyond man's control. Popular superstition created a god who oversaw all the marriages; he was sometimes called the Old Man in the Moon. Temples were dedicated to him in different parts of the country and people went there to seek advice from the oracles and diviners about their marriages. This old story is about a man who actually met the God of Marriage.

Once in the Tang dynasty there was a man by the name of Wei whose parents died when he was quite young. When he grew up he was eager to get married and have a family, to compensate for the one that he had lost in childhood, but as he had no parents to help him make a match, families with marriagable girls were suspicious of him and to his great disappointment he could not find a wife. One day as he was travelling he arrived at a city called Song where he stayed at an inn. There he met a man of the town and as they talked, Wei explained his difficulties. The man suggested that the daughter of the town marshal might be a suitable match for Wei and he offered to speak to the marshal for him. The two men arranged to meet again the next day early in the morning in front of a temple near the inn.

Since Wei was very anxious, he arrived at the temple very early indeed while the pale moon was still in the sky, before dawn had broken. On the steps in front of the temple Wei saw an old man sitting with his back against a sack, reading a book by the light of the moon. Wei approached and glanced over his shoulder at the book but found that he could not read a single word. To him, the writing looked more like some kind of beetle track than Chinese characters. With his curiosity aroused, he asked the old man, 'Sir, what kind of book is that that you are looking at? Since I was a child I have studied many languages and can read several different kinds of writing, including

years, winning many battles and becoming famous for his skill and courage. Eventually, however, he was captured by the king's enemies. Knowing what a valuable ally he would make, they tried in every way they could to persuade him to change sides. But Guan Yü remained loyal, and chose to die at the hand of his enemies rather than betray his king.

scripts from the Western Lands of India, but I have never in my life seen a book like yours.'

The old man smiled and said 'You could not have seen a book like this. It is not a mortal book.'

'How can that be?' asked Wei.

'It is a book from the Underworld.'

'If you are from the other world, what are you doing here?' asked Wei.

The old man looked around him before he replied. Then he said, 'You are up very early,' and paused. Finally he replied, 'Usually there is no-one about except people like us. We people from the Underworld who are in charge of the affairs of men must now and then walk about among human beings. Often we do our walking in the dim half light of the early dawn.'

By now Wei's curiosity was thoroughly aroused and he decided to find out as much as he could. 'What is it that you are in charge of?' he asked.

The old man replied, 'I'm in charge of marriages.'

Wei was delighted at this coincidence and saw his chance to take advantage of it. 'I have been alone in the world since my childhood and have wanted to get married and have a family of my own for a long time. For ten years now I have tried to find a suitable wife but with no success. Now I hope to be able to marry the marshal's daughter. Tell me, will my marriage succeed?'

The old man looked into his book and after a while he replied, 'No. She is not the person destined for you. Your wife is only three years old at the moment. When she is seventeen, she will marry you.'

Wei was very disappointed, thinking that it would be a very long time for him to wait. Then he noticed the sack against which the old man was leaning. 'What is inside your sack?' he asked and the old man replied, 'Red thread for tying the feet of husbands and wives. You cannot see it but once they are tied they can never be separated. They are already linked with my thread to one another at birth and it does not matter how wide a gulf separates them, whether their families are enemies, their position in society wide apart or their homes in different countries, sooner or later they will come together as man and wife. Once the red thread is tied there is no way of cutting it.

Your foot has already been tied to that of your future wife so there is no point in struggling against it.'

At this Wei became very excited. 'Where is my wife now? What does her family do?'

The old man replied very calmly, 'She is not far from here and she is the daughter of old Mother Chen, the market stall keeper.'

'Can I see her?'

'Yes if you insist. Mother Chen always brings her when she sells vegetables and fruit at the market. If you really want to see her, you can come with me and I will show you, but remember it will make no difference to your future.'

Wei was still eager, so the old man put his book away into the sack and stood up. By now it was dawn, and as the man Wei had hoped to meet had not yet arrived, Wei followed the old man to the market in a state of some excitement.

The market was filling up with the morning crowd of stall-keepers and shoppers. Behind a tumble-down stall of fruit and vegetables stood a poor looking old woman who was blind in one eye. She was carrying a little girl who looked about three years old and both of them were clothed in the filthiest of rags.

'There is your wife,' said the old man, pointing to the little girl. Wei felt disgust and anger rising up in him and he said, 'What if I killed her?'

The old man looked at him. 'She is destined to enjoy riches and high rank and the respect of her family. Whatever you do it will make no difference to her fate.' With these words the old man disappeared.

Wei cursed, 'You meddlesome demon from hell! My family is a noble one and the girl I marry will be my equal in birth. If I can't marry a noble woman then I shall find the most beautiful geisha girl and make her my wife instead. Why should I marry some ragamuffin beggar with a blind mother?'

Wei left the market in a furious anger, full of murderous intentions. He found a small knife and sharpened it until it was razor keen. Then he handed it to his slave boy saying, 'You have always been good at carrying out my orders. Now go and kill this girl for me and I'll reward you with ten thousand pieces of copper.'

The slave boy took the knife. The next day he

hid it in his sleeve and went to the market. He mingled with the crowd and gradually worked his way towards the old blind woman and the little girl. Swiftly he pulled out his knife, stabbed the child, turned and ran away. The market place was full of screams, panic and confusion and in the crowd the boy escaped and made his way back to his master.

'Did you get her?' asked Wei and the boy replied, 'I tried to stab her in the heart but I hit her between the eyes.' The boy received his reward and his release from slavery and Wei, relieved that he was now free to marry, continued as before. In time he forgot the whole affair.

Wei's efforts to find a suitable wife continued to be unsuccessful and when fourteen years had passed he was still unmarried. That year he was working at a place called Shiangzhou, and he was doing very well there. His superior, the governor of the area, was impressed by his ability and offered his daughter to him as a suitable wife. So at last Wei had a wife of good birth and beautiful appearance. She was just seventeen years old and Wei was delighted and loved her dearly.

As soon as he met her Wei noticed that his wife always wore a patch on her forehead and after they were married he discovered that she never removed it even when she washed or slept. He did not ask her about it but it continued to worry him and he could not stop thinking about it. Then, several years later, he suddenly remembered the incident with his slave boy and the little girl in the market place and he decided to ask his wife about the patch. Weeping, his wife told him, 'I am not the real daughter of the Governor of Shiangzhou, but his niece. My father was once the governor of a city called Song and he died there. I was still a baby when my mother and brother died there too. My nurse, Mrs Chen, took pity on me and looked after me. When I was three years old she took me with her to the market and I was stabbed by some madman. The scar of his knife is still here so I always cover it up with a patch. About seven or eight years ago my uncle returned from the south and took me to live with him. Then he married me to you as his daughter.'

'Was Mrs Chen blind in one eye?' Wei asked.

His wife was astonished. 'Yes', she said, 'how did you know?'

'It was I that tried to have you killed,' said Wei greatly moved. 'How strange is destiny.'

Then he told his wife the whole story and now that they both knew the truth they loved each other all the more. Later they had a son who became a high official and they were greatly honored in their old age.

Where the stories come from

The early myths of China dealing with the creation of the world, the gods and heroes, have come down to us in a fragmentary state: some of the stories can only be pieced together from references made to them in ancient texts such as the works of Taoist philosophy, a collection of early poetry dating from the fourth century BC called the *Songs of Chu (Chuci)* and a book of mythical cosmography called the *Classic of Mountains and Seas (Shanhaijing)*. Most of this has been collected in a scholarly work called *Ancient Chinese Mythology (Zhongguo gudai shen hua)* by Yüan Ke (published in Shanghai in 1951).

In the sixth century tales of marvellous happenings were very popular and many of the collections contain versions of early myths as well as contemporary folk tales. One well known collection was *The Book of Seeking Immortals (Sou shen ji)*, from which come stories in this volume such as *Panhu the marvellous dog*, *The silkworm*, *The haunted pavilion* and others.

This tradition continued and several hundred years later scholars of the Tang dynasty in the ninth century wrote some vivid and realistic short stories using themes from mythology and folklore; they were known as *Legends of Marvels (Chuanqi)*. From their works I have taken *The story of Liu Yi*, *The world in a pillow*, *The story of Lady Ren* and *The god of marriage*.

The religious tale of Mulien, written by an anonymous author, was preserved in the archives of the Dunhuang monastery to the far west of China, on the old silk route. The story was written in a form popular amongst Buddhists and influenced by a form of Sanskrit literature called *bianwen*. *Bianwen* was written in a mixture of verse and prose and it became the dominant format for popular literature. Some works, particularly religious stories, were exclusively in verse, and were called *baojuan*. This was the form in which the legend of Miaoshan, told here in *Guanyin the Goddess of Mercy*, has been found. Anonymous ballads based on popular legends also made their appearance, such as the story of Meng Jiangnu. Popular fiction later tended to be written predominantly in prose. An example is the story of Lady White which was written in a more literary style by a writer called Feng Menglong (died 1646) who wrote several collections of popular tales.

The story of the Monkey Spirit comes from a Ming dynasty source, a full-length novel put together by a writer named Wu Cheng-en (died 1582) called the *Journey to the West (Xi you ji)* and containing elements of folklore current at the time. The legend of Tripitaka was based on an historical figure who left China for India in 640 AD. When he returned home with the scriptures he later became a leading figure in Chinese Buddhism.

Many other novels based on folklore and legend also first made their appearance in the Ming. The Prince Nocha story comes from a novel of about the same period called *The Romance of the Making of Gods (Feng shen yenyi)*. The later Ming dynasty works show a distinct difference in style and content from the earlier folktales and legends, in their greater colourfulness and their love of magic and supernatural displays.

The sources

A Dictionary of Chinese Mythology, E. T. C. Werner: Stove god (p. 120); Door gods and gods of the elements (p. 121).
Beijing di chuanshuo: Gaoling Bridge (p. 49).
Dong Yong Chen Xiang ji: Dong Yong, the faithful son (p. 114)
Dunhuang bianwen ji ed. Xiang Ta et. al.: Mulien rescues his mother (p. 64); The monk Huiyuan (p. 70).
Feng shen yenyi: Prince Nocha (p. 74).
Guan Yü xi ji: Lord Guan (p. 126).
Hua Yang Guo Zhi: The cuckoo (p. 24).
Jingshi tongyen 'Bainiangzi yongzhen leifengta': Lady White (p. 87).
Liaozhai zhiyi 'Hejian sheng': The man from Hejian (p. 83).
Meng Jiangnu wanli xun fu ji: The story of Meng Jiangnu (p. 109).
Researches into Chinese Superstitions, Henri Doré. vols. VI, IX: The eight immortals (p. 81); Gods of the stars (p. 124).
Shanhaijing: Kuafu chases the sun (p. 19); The giant without a head (p. 20); The bird and the sea (p. 22).
Shen xian zhuan: Zhang Daoling (p. 76).
Shiji, 'Sanhuang benji': Nüwa mends heaven (p. 17).
Shijing, Daya: The child abandoned on the ice (p. 34).
Shu Yi Ji: The Yellow Emperor (p. 20).
Sou shen ji: Panhu, the marvellous dog (p. 38); The crane maiden (p. 39); The silkworm (p. 45); The haunted pavilion (p. 85): The swordmaker's son (p. 116); The night bird (p. 86).
Taiping Guangji 291: Li Bing fights the river god (p. 37).
Tang Xiaoshuo 'Ding hun dian': The god of marriage (p. 127).
    'Liu Yi Zhuan': Liu Yi and the dragon king (p. 53).
    'Ren shi zhuan': Lady Ren (p. 92).
    'Zhentou ji': The world in a pillow (p. 71).
The Legend of Miaoshan, G. Dudbridge: The story of Guanyin (p. 60).
Xi you ji: The Monkey spirit (p. 96).
Xin xi qu, II, 5: The herd boy and the ox (p. 41).
Zhongguo di shuishen, Hang Zhigang: The dragon's pearl (p. 58).
Zhongguo gudai shen hua, Yüan Ke: Pangu (p. 13); Nüwa creates man (p. 15); Isles of the blest (p. 18); Yi the archer (p. 25); Chang'o and the Elixir of Immortality (p. 29); Yü controls the flood (p. 32); Shun the wise emperor (p. 35).

Symbols in the Chinese myths

At the beginning of each chapter the artist has illustrated some of the symbols which are identified with the themes or characters in the stories.

p. 11 THE CHINESE WORLD Chinese characters were written with brushes of different thicknesses, dipped in ink. The crane and the pine are symbols of long life. The lotus lamp is a Buddhist symbol, here representing one of the major Chinese religions.

p. 13 GODS FROM THE DAWN OF TIME One of the earliest gods, the mother goddess Nüwa.

p. 25 THE EARLY HEROES The bow and quiver full of arrows belong to Yi, with the sun that remained after he had shot down its brothers. The dragon is a traditional decorative motif. Below, the horse-drawn carriage is a warrior's chariot. The background pattern is a characteristic design, often found on woodwork and silk.

p. 37 WHEN GODS AND MEN MINGLED The crane into which the Crane Maiden changed for her visits to earth; the herd boy and his ox—the spirit of the ox star; the horse who changed into a silk worm.

p. 48 THE CHINESE DRAGONS Chinese dragons were associated with water and were often the guardian spirits of lakes and rivers. Normally dragons had four claws but the imperial dragon had five on each foot. The dragon's magic pearl was its most prized possession.

p. 60 BUDDHIST TALES Pagodas were built to contain sacred relics. The Buddha is shown in his traditional pose.

p. 73 TAOIST TALES OF MAGIC AND FANTASY Laozi, the author of the *Tao Te Ching*. He carries a scroll inscribed with the Taoist symbols for the masculine and femine principles, yin and yang. The deer symbolizes the Taoist's affinity with nature; the gourd contains the elixir of immortality.

p. 83 SPIRITS AND DEMONS Animal spirits often appeared as beautiful young women, usually, though not always with malicious intentions.

p. 96 THE MONKEY SPIRIT Tripitaka on his dragon horse; the Hog of the Eight Abstinences with his rake; Sandman priest with a halberd and Monkey with his magic stick.

p. 109 TALES OF FAITH AND LOYALTY The sword Ganjiang; a scroll made of bamboo strips, used for writing before the invention of paper, representing Dong Yong's studious achievements; and a temple to symbolize spiritual aspirations.

p. 120 GODS AND SUPERSTITIONS The door god, one of a pair of images hung outside the house door to protect the inmates from danger; incense and incense sticks used in popular worship. The characters on the bowl read 'luck'.

Characters and symbols in the illustrations

p. 16-17 Fushi drew up the eight hexagrams used in divination, later interpreted in a manual known as the *Yching* or Book of Changes. The picture, based on an illustration from the Sung dynasty, by Ma Lin, shows Fushi and the tortoise traditionally used. Fushi's long nails are characteristic of scholars. The tortoise was killed and the divisions into which its shell cracked were interpreted and written down. The eight hexagrams are:

Heaven	☰	mountains	☶
Earth	☷	storm	☳
water	☵	marshland	☱
fire	☲	wind	☴

p. 99 Buddha's hand is inscribed 'Great sage, equal of Heaven'.

p. 120 The characters read 'luck'.

p. 129 Traditional marriage costume. The bride wears a phoenix diadem, symbolizing the yin or feminine principle. The room wears a scholar's cap (academic robes were often worn for weddings). The feathers in his cap could only be worn by those who had passed their examinations with the highest distinction. The traditional colour for weddings is red. The symbol is the character 'married happiness' written twice. This is always used as a decoration on invitations, utensils, wall hangings etc. for wedding ceremonies.

Index

131